→52←
WAYS
TO·BE·A
BETTER
STEP-
PARENT

Bl. Family
OLO

1247

⟫52⟪

WAYS

TO · BE · A

BETTER
STEP-
PARENT

O'Connor & Flowers

Publishers Since 1798

THOMAS NELSON PUBLISHERS
NASHVILLE

Published in Nashville, Tennessee, by Thomas Nelson, Inc., Publishers, and distributed in Canada by Word Communications, Ltd., Richmond, British Columbia, and in the Untied Kingdom by Word (UK), Ltd., Milton Keynes, England.

Scripture quotations are from the NEW KING JAMES VERSION of the Bible. Copyright © 1979, 1980, 1982, Thomas Nelson, Inc., Publishers.

Library of Congress Cataloging-in-Publications Data

O'Connor, Karen, 1938-
   52 ways to be a better stepparent / Karen O'Connor and Charles Flowers.
     p. cm.
   ISBN 0-8407-3442-5 (pbk)
   1. Stepparents — United States. 2. Parent and child — United States. 3. Creative activities and seat work. I. Flowers, Charles, 1928- . II Title. III. Title:Fifty-two ways to be a better stepparent.
HQ759.92.025 1993
306.874 — dc20   92-44729
                                                   CIP

Printed in the United States of America
1 2 3 4 5 6 7 – 98 97 96 95 94 93

Dedicated to
our children and stepchildren:
Julie, Jim, and Erin
Cliff and Cathy

Introduction

As the formerly married marry again and bring their natural children into the new relationship, everyone involved is suddenly thrust into a new experience — "the blended family."

Blending adults, natural children, and stepchildren under one roof, and relating to various members of the extended families, is a challenge, especially for the children who probably didn't have much to say about their parents' decision to remarry.

But a blending of two families occurs even if the children do not live in the same household with the parent who remarries. Since they generally spend weekends, holidays, or extended summer visits with their natural parent and new stepparent, they too, need opportunities and activities that provide a sense of belonging.

And when a child's natural mother and father both remarry, he or she must then find a rightful place in two blended families — which include stepparents, stepsiblings, stepgrandparents, and others on both sides. Building and managing all these relationships can result in stress for everyone.

Stepparents face the challenge of being sensitive to their own children in a new way, as well as responding with love to their step-children, providing both with the freedom to *blend* at their own rate of comfort and safety.

If children are later born of the new relationship, the blending takes on still another dimension. Meanwhile, the adults in the household also have one another to think of!

This adds up to a tall order for anyone. But the blending can occur.

Many parents and children attest to the success of their blended families when they really get involved in each others' lives.

It is not enough simply to *talk* about the problems and the needs, however. It's vital for parents and children to *do* things together — to play games, to pray, to participate in family projects or learn new skills, to be involved in gift-buying and giving, to have a voice in financial decisions, and vote at family meetings.

52 Ways to Be a Better Stepparent offers a variety of activities and events that will help you give and receive nurturing, provide each member of your blended family an experience of belonging, share communication, laughter, and fun, create a history together, and build a strong base of love and mutual acceptance.

Don't feel discouraged if you can't do all of them or if some don't fit your lifestyle or family situation. They are meant as suggestions — ideas to consider and experiment with. Feel free to adapt them to the particular needs, ages, and interests of your family. We have found that they apply whether you are together under the same roof, share only a few hours a week or a couple of weeks a year, and whether your children are toddlers, teens, or adults.

CONTENTS

COMMUNICATION

1 ◆ Connect with Your Stepchildren

It takes time for stepparents to really know their stepchildren. But you can shorten that learning process with an entertaining and informative excercise in list-making. All you need is paper and pencil. Gather around a table or curl up on some big pillows on the floor. Give each family member his or her own paper and pencil.

What to Do Assemble a list of topics on a chalkboard or poster (use the list suggested here or modify it to suit your family). Ask each person to choose one category and write it at the top of a page, and then list their preferences. Afterward, invite responses. One person might want to share his entire list. Someone else may prefer to share only some of the entries. Allow each one to share at his or her comfort level. Go around again, this time choosing a new topic. Continue for a set time or until interest fades. Repeat the process at another time. Keep the lists in an album or scrapbook and invite other family members, such as grandparents, stepgrandparents, aunts, uncles, and cousins, to add to them when they visit. Not only will you gain insight into the individual children, but you may notice some generational patterns. For example, likes and dislikes for particular foods or activities are often passed on. Musical talent, writing ability, and so on frequently show up on the lists of both parent and child, providing more information about your spouse as well as stepchildren.

- My three favorite books
- My favorite foods
- Places I like to go
- Three ways to be a good friend
- My favorite kind of music
- What I like to do when I'm alone
- What I like to do when I'm with others
- Places I want to visit
- Hobbies and games I like to play

Keep Going If you want to take it a step further, make lists of specific items such as: toys, nursery rhymes, sports figures, musical instruments, songs, childhood books. Then compare them with preferences from a year ago. Talk about how some of the changes occurred and what you expect in the future.

Suggest Alternatives If some of the children are too young to write, have them speak their lists into a tape recorder or ask another family member to write them. The child can draw pictures to illustrate the lists. Another option is for one family member to compose a list for another member to see how much each knows about the other's preferences. This could spark a lively discussion.

Another time you might wish to list things you don't like, and then talk about why you dislike them. The purpose of this activity is not to dwell on the negative, but to assure your stepchildren that there is room in your family for more than one way of expressing individuality.

2 ◆ Share Memories

Some children in blended families feel they have to pretend their other parents and families don't exist in order to fit into the new structure. This can be a damaging experience for both the children and the stepparent. Over time denying the truth will break down, creating resentment and anger. You can help your stepchildren deal with conflicts of loyalty by encouraging them to openly share the details of their "other" life. You can do the same, modeling this behavior for them, and in doing so, you will help them experience safety in coming to you with future difficult communications.

How It Works Sit in a circle on the floor or in chairs to create an atmosphere of closeness and safety. Tell everyone that nothing is off-limits in this sharing period. It's all right to talk about any detail even if it involves someone who is not part of the current blended family. Start with one unfinished sentence from the following list (or from a list you've created). Take turns finishing the sentence and then move on to the next one. Move through the list for a period of time that feels right or stretch out the list over several weeks. Remind everyone to pay attention and listen quietly to each other.

- I remember feeling really happy in my other family (with my mom or dad, or with my ex-husband or ex-wife) when . . .
- I remember being angry when . . .
- One of the happiest Christmases in my other family was . . .
- I felt really scared when . . .

- I felt the most lonely when . . .
- I remember a sad time when our family . . .
- The thing I like best about my other family is . . .
- The thing I like best about this family is . . .

Another Angle Write the unfinished sentences on individual slips of paper and drop them in a basket or shoe box. Each family member draws one out and responds.

This would also make a good quiet game while traveling in a car or when some children seem particularly sullen or moody. Often they just need to talk.

3 ◆ Talk About What's Important

Your blended family, like other families, probably is a melting pot of ages, opinions, backgrounds, preferences, emotions. Only yours is all the more a mix because of the history that each one brings to the new structure. To create a close and lasting bond with your stepchildren — especially adolescents and teenagers — look for opportunities to seek out their viewpoint and values on a variety of topics.

Plan Ahead Use 12 index cards or cut paper into as many 4 inch by 6 inch pieces. On one side of each write, "This is how I feel about . . ." On the other side write one of the following phrases, or make up your own:

- families that go through a divorce
- my mother or father dating a new person
- having a stepbrother or stepsister
- having a different last name from the one some of the people in my family have
- having a bigger family than I did before
- having to share my parents with their stepchildren
- living with a stepparent
- visiting my other parent on weekends and vacations
- sharing my room when (name of stepsibling) visits
- our family meetings
- going to church as a family

- doing this activity

Getting Started Sit across from each other in a circle or at the family table. Ask one person to choose a card and respond. Then pass it around and let each one who wishes respond in turn. Members may choose to remain silent. Some children will participate freely after observing a round or two. Encourage everyone to accept each person's answer. The idea is to "get" what he or she says, not to judge, criticize, or attempt to change it.

Another time you might turn over the card-writing task to one of the older children. That exercise in itself could be very revealing. Once family members feel comfortable with the routine, consider focusing on issues outside the home such as politics, the environment, entertainment, school, friendships, clothing, food preferences, and so on.

4 ♦ Clear the Air with a Heart Talk

Life is a challenge. Communication breakdowns, hurt feelings, special needs, individual viewpoints, differing ages, temperaments, and backgrounds all play a part in the dynamics of living together. But members of a blended family seem to be especially threatened by the expression of negative feelings. Loyalty conflicts spring up. Relationships are jealously guarded. Individuals pit themselves against others and often refuse to talk about what's bothering them.

You can help yourself, your spouse, and most of all, your stepchildren with an exercise that will stimulate and encourage each member of your family to express his or her negative feelings in an arena of safety and acceptance.

Getting to the Heart of the Matter Ahead of time, cut a piece of construction paper in the shape of a heart. On a piece of paper or poster board, list the following partial sentences about family life (or make up your own):

- I feel angry when . . .
- I hate it when . . .
- I feel unhappy when . . .
- I feel jealous when . . .
- I wish our family didn't have to . . .
- I don't like it when I have to . . .

- I don't like it when (name the person) tells me . . .
- Something I'd like to change is . . .
- If I were the mother (or father) in this family I would . . .
- I feel like no one loves me when . . .

Pass the Heart, Please! Sit in a circle on the floor. Model a few sentences so the children will hear how to share their feelings responsibly — without blaming or ridiculing anyone. For example, it would be okay to say, "I feel angry when Jenny plays with my doll collection when I'm not home." It would not be okay to say, "I feel angry when dumb Jenny trashes my dolls when I'm not home to stop her."

Start with one person holding the heart. Ask him or her to choose one partial sentence from the list, say it out loud, and then finish it. Everyone else listens. When that person is finished, he or she passes the heart to the person on the left and so on until everyone has had a chance to complete the same phrase. Select another person and another phrase and repeat the process as many times as you wish. The important factor here is the opportunity to express negative feelings freely without fear of being corrected or admonished when the process is over.

Go Deeper Still Afterward invite family members to repeat at least one thing they heard during the exercise. This will give parents and children an additional opportunity to express caring and to sharpen listening skills.

5 ♦ Make a Blessing Box

A blessing box (or bag) is a great way to notice and acknowledge God's daily gifts. An unused shoe or tissue box or a bag with a handle will do. You can use it as is or decorate and title it "Our Blessing Box" or "Our Blessing Bag."

Place the box or bag in a strategic place where the family gathers for meals or entertainment, usually the kitchen, dining room, or family room. Place a pad of note paper or a box of paper scraps and a pen or pencil nearby. At the end of a meal you might ask, "Does anyone want to add something to the blessing box?"

Individuals then jot down on one of the note papers the date and the blessing received, and drop it into the box or bag whenever they wish. On one appointed day each month or at the end of the year, gather round, open the box, and take turns reading the blessings aloud. This activity will draw you close as a family, turn your thoughts to God as the author of all blessings, and help everyone focus on the positive elements in your family life.

We like to start a new blessing box each January 1. We accumulate the papers for the entire year. Then on New Year's Eve we read them aloud and give thanks again for all the ways God blessed us during the year. It increases our faith in prayer and our recognition of God's ever-present grace in our lives. It can also be a powerful way of teaching children about God's provision and protection and can serve as an opportunity for spiritual intimacy within your blended family.

Taking Action   When family members focus on their blessings instead of on their burdens, a new level of love and understanding develops almost effortlessly. Hostility, jealousy, and quibbling among the children diminish naturally as family members come together to talk about their blessings, to write them down, and to share them again at a later time.

This family project takes little time, but the benefits are enormous. As members of a household talk about their experiences over breakfast or dinner, it will be apparent to everyone how many blessings they've received even in the course of one day: protection in travel, help with tests at school, guidance during a meeting at work, favors done for one another, money for needed purchases, peace of mind in a difficult relationship.

Deep healing between stepparents and stepchildren can also result from this simple exercise. When you voice, in the presence of the entire family, a blessing you received through one of your stepchildren, a number of things occur. First, speaking directly to the child validates him or her. Second, you contribute to a healthy self-image by acknowledging him or her in front of others. And third, you reinforce positive, caring behavior. Of course this is effective with other members of the family, as well, but is especially powerful between stepparent and stepchildren where this level of communication is more the exception than the norm.

Think of the results that would come about over such simple statements as these: "Ann, thanks for folding the laundry. That was a blessing." "I was blessed, Peter, when you took the time to call me at work today." "What a blessing, Bobby and Chris, to come home and find you had started dinner for us."

Variations on the Theme
   • Start a blessing box for family blessings, individual blessings,

or examples of answered prayer. Open and read on a monthly, quarterly, or yearly basis.

- Give to another family an empty blessing box as a gift, complete with note paper and pen, and instructions for how to use it.
- Stuff a blessing bag with prayers of thanks for a friend or family member and give it as a birthday, anniversary, or get-well gift.
- Make a large blessing box for your church or several small ones for individual Sunday school classes. At the end of the year, have a party. Ask each participant to take a blessing from the box and read it aloud. Celebrate with a time of thanksgiving and worship, followed by refreshments.

6 ◆ Pray with One Another

Prayer is probably one of the most challenging aspects of family life — especially in blended families, where the traditions, viewpoints, and practices of individuals may differ. How do parents get everyone together at the same time for prayer? How can these times meet the needs of each individual, especially when those individuals range from babies to adults? Should the prayers be formal or conversational? Should prayer times include a Scripture reading or a short daily meditation?

Some families start family prayer time enthusiastically only to have it fizzle out after a few nights. Crying babies, restless toddlers, evening commitments, homework, different bedtimes and a host of other distractions get in the way of a meaningful time of prayer. Our suggestion? Don't fight it. Find a new way to pray — a way that works for you and your household.

Pray Without Ceasing — What That Means First of all, consider your entire life a life of prayer. There are, of course, times of quiet where you attend to prayer only, but there are countless other moments during the day where you can "toss" up prayers to the Lord as you write a report at work, change a baby's diaper, prepare a meal, drive to the store, or stand in the line at the post office.

You don't have to confine yourself to formal times of prayer or to times of formal prayer. You can get in the habit of speaking to the Lord spontaneously throughout the day — and night, if you awaken. These ongoing conversations will gradually become a part of you.

As you become more comfortable with spontaneous prayer you will naturally teach this way of praying to your stepchildren. You will help them associate prayer with every activity in their lives rather than limiting prayer to set times that sometimes feel forced.

Creative Family Prayer There are many ways you can have a time of prayer that involves the entire family or just you and one of your stepchildren.

MEALTIME
- One person leads and the others pray silently.
- Take turns saying one thing you are grateful for.
- Say a mealtime prayer together.

BEDTIME
- Trace the sign of the cross on your children's foreheads and ask God to bless them as they sleep.
- Pray a short informal prayer aloud together before sleeping.
- Pray over your stepchildren while they sleep.

ILLNESSES
- Lay hands on the sick and pray for healing.
- Share aloud healing Scriptures with the sick person.
- Create a prayer card, listing three or four healing Scriptures.

DEPARTURES and ABSENCES
- Hold hands and pray for protection for those leaving the home.
- Agree on an appointed time to pray for one another while separated.

PRAYER PARTNERSHIPS
- Pair up for a day or a week or longer and pray for one another's

special needs during that specified period. (This is another good way to strengthen ties in your blended family. Pair up a child with an adult, a stepparent with a stepchild, a child with a child, and so on.)

HOUSE BLESSING

- As a family, walk through your house and around your property and automobiles, and pray for protection over your dwelling and possessions. (We have found this is a good reminder that all these things belong to God and we are mere stewards, relying on Him for guidance and protection.)

PRAYER NOTES

- Tuck a prayer note in your stepchild's lunch bag.
- Slip a prayer of support into a textbook for your stepchild who is studying for a test.
- Place a prayer note under a pillow or in a pocket.

PRAYER CIRCLE

- Gather as a family in a circle to pray in the morning, at night, or whenever you feel led. One person can lead and the others follow. Or each person can express a need and the person to his or her right will pray for that stated need.

Whatever your need or desire, take it to the Lord in prayer for "he heareth the prayer of the righteous." (Prov. 15:29)

7 ◆ Compile a Blended Family History

History on Tape Over the years, a friend of ours tape-recorded conversations during visits with distant or elderly relatives. It was her way of preserving her memories of them and passing a part of her family heritage on to her children. Now that four of those people have died, she is listening to the tapes as she writes a memoir of her life growing up in a Jewish family.

A man in one of Karen's classes said he spent many hours during the latter part of his mother's life tape-recording her oral history of her early years homesteading in New Mexico. He has since turned his notes and her story into an article that was recently published in *New Mexico Magazine*. He hopes one day to expand the article into a book.

Tape-recording is just one of the ways you can document portions of your family life and those of prior generations. You can transfer some of the stories into written form, or use parts as captions under photographs. Or you can include them in a narrative that links one generation to another through photos, mementos, news clips, awards, merit badges, and so on.

You can be as elaborate or as simple as you wish. You could just jot down significant family events in each decade. Or you could write a kind of family diary, making periodic entries whenever you're moved to do so.

History on Paper One mother keeps a written history of each of her children starting with birth. Each history is in the form of a letter, in which she tells the child her thoughts, feelings, observations, and wishes for him or her during each year. She adds to the letter whenever she wants to. Sometimes a milestone triggers her desire to write. Other times she jots down her thoughts and feelings as they arise.

This is something each of the natural parents in a blended family can do for his or her children. What a gift! And what a special way for children to weave the various parts of their life together. Stepparents can add to it, as well.

History in a Scrapbook Children can participate in putting together a family or individual history. When they reach school age, help them assemble important documents, photos, and memorabilia in a scrapbook and add written comments as they are able.

Encourage them to write their observations and reflections after family vacations or shared holidays or any time that seems appropriate.

History on a Wall The Winter family has lined the stairway walls of their home with photo collages of their family through the years. One can see at a glance the people, places, and events that have played a part in the life of this family. Ellen Winter supplied appropriate captions and Ed Winter arranged the photos by decades. Beginning at the turn of the century with the great-grandparents, the Winters now have a visual history of more than eight decades, including a few choice photos of their children and themselves before Ed and Ellen joined their families through their marriage ten years ago.

However you choose to create your family history is less important than actually doing it. Even if you don't have much to go on, work with what you have and go forward. You will be providing your children and stepchildren with a gift that can never be replaced and they will be the richer for it.

8 ♦ Lend a Helping Hand

Everyone can use a helping hand! And what better environment than a family for teaching and learning the art of helping one another. Lending a hand is a real opportunity for stepparents, in particular, to display their care and affection for their stepchildren.

Getting Started Here's a way to make it fun and specific. You can initiate it, then incorporate it into your entire family life.

1. Buy a bulletin board or clear a space on the one you already have.
2. Stack some sheets of plain white paper and a pencil or marking pen on a table nearby.
3. Trace one of your hands on one of the sheets of paper, like the example on page 18.
4. Fill in each finger with a task you're willing to help with, such as: math homework, pet feeding, working a puzzle, carrying out the trash, or delivering newspapers. You could also leave one finger blank so the user can fill in his or her choice.
5. At the top of the page write the words "Need A Hand? Call me. I have an extra one!"
6. Pin your page to the family bulletin board whenever you are available for service. It might be once a day, once a week, once a month, or whenever.
7. Let the kids know you're willing to lend a hand for the specified chores or for the one of their choice if they choose the blank finger.

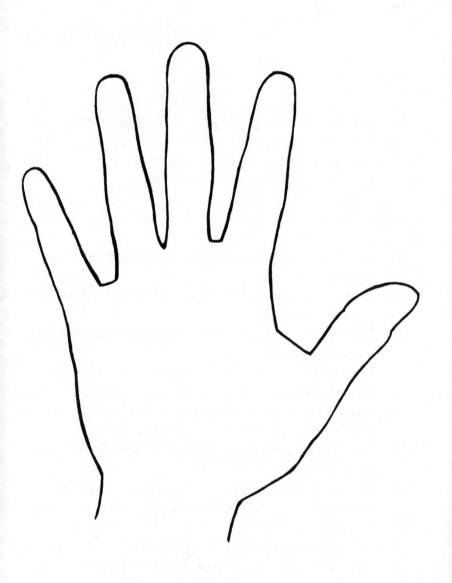

This activity doesn't replace helping kids in the usual way such as bathing toddlers, driving them to appointments, listening to them after school, reading bedtime stories, and so forth. It is an "extra," covering activities and chores kids usually expect to do without assistance.

If this activity catches on in your family, you can then encourage everyone to participate so that children and adults are all lending hands to one another.

More Ways to Help You could also vary the activities:

1. Create a helping-hand box and put it in the room where your family gather most. Trace a hand on a sheet of blank paper and make copies. Let each family member fill out one and place it on the bulletin board as he or she wants to.

2. Put out a box of blank sheets. Encourage family members to choose one when they wish, trace their hands, write in the help they can offer or leave it blank (for the person in need to choose what he or she wants) and put it on the bulletin board.

3. Create helping-hand gifts. You could create, decorate, and give a group of helping hands as gifts to your stepchildren and others. Wrap one up and put it in a box. Tuck one inside a tennis shoe or under a pillow. Hide one in a lunch box. It's another great way to say "I care about you and I want to help."

9 ◆ Establish a Family Fun Fund

Alice says she grew up in her stepfather's household feeling deprived. "It seemed there was never enough money for me — for the things I wanted. My mother made me go to him for all my financial needs. I hated it. He was nice to me in most ways, but he was so tight with money. I felt that even little things, like a pair of sandals or a new hair ribbon, were out of reach."

Many adults recall similar backgrounds where one parent handled all financial decisions and everyone in the family had to "make a good case for what they needed," as one man put it.

Now picture a different scenario — a home where children as well as adults participate in financial discussions and decisions. Children learn to handle money responsibly, and parents and stepparents could find out from the kids themselves what they need and want and then talk about how to pay for them.

If you want to improve your relationship with your stepchildren in this area, consider establishing a fund for family fun. You can use this tool to create good feelings and positive responses to money management. You could plan your saving strategy at a monthly or quarterly family meeting. Talk about Christmas spending, family vacation, camp, tickets for concerts and athletic events, sporting equipment, and so on. There are a number of ways to handle this, but the important thing is to get started. You can refine the process as you go along.

Open a Special Savings Account The Redding family has established one of their savings accounts as the Family Fund. Each month the parents deposit one hundred dollars from their paychecks. This money goes toward a family vacation during the summer. Each of the four children (ranging from ten to sixteen years of age) contributes a part of his or her weekly allowance, baby-sitting money, and newspaper delivery earnings to the fund each week. The amount fluctuates based on age and earnings. The parents supervise the management of the fund and help the children make responsible choices.

In this situation, however, the parents, are the primary contributors, as they should be. But since the children participate as well, everyone shares in making decisions about how and where to spend the money. This democratic process helps to quell rivalry between family members.

Many blended families have a poor balance between power and authority. For example, if the primary earner is the dad, then the stepchildren may feel he will favor his own children over them. This creates rivalry and resentment. Or if both parents work, and the children go to their natural parent with financial needs, one may be able to afford more than the other. The children in the home feel this inequity.

By establishing a family fund, everyone participates and everyone's needs and wants are considered.

Set Up a Petty Cash Fund Suppose you do open a designated savings account, but you prefer to keep it intact for major purchases such as a tent, or a plane trip to visit relatives, or a family vacation to Disney-World. If that's the case, then how do you handle the small, weekly entertainment needs such as concert or movie tickets, a day at the zoo, or a hike in the mountains?

You can establish a petty cash fund or use the envelope system, and set aside a percentage of earnings for weekly entertainment needs. And what do you do if one person wants to attend the symphony and another a hockey game? You can handle this by allowing individuals to have access to a certain portion of the fund for the things they enjoy. For example, a toddler would probably be satisfied with a small book. A teenager might want a phone for his room. If they want more than the system allows, they can earn the extra money needed.

Suppose your twelve-year-old stepdaughter asks to attend a community fair. The ticket is $5. She's already used up her portion of the family fund for this month. What can you do? First, talk it over with her. Show her the numbers in your ledger. Then brainstorm ways for her to earn the money by doing extra chores around the house, babysitting, or working for a neighbor.

There is no *one* way to approach this. Your stepchildren may have some ideas you haven't thought of. The important thing is to let them know that together you are a family and each one is valued and loved. There is both time and money for you to share fun with one another and with friends.

10 ◆ Take a Class Together

Ten-year-old Amy and her stepmom, Jan, are enrolled in an art class together. Amy has been drawing since she was in pre-school. When Jan met Amy she was reminded of her own interest in art as a child. After Jan married Amy's father, she suggested she and Amy take a class together at the art museum. "It has drawn us closer," said Jan. "I think Amy is beginning to believe that I really care about her; that I'm here for her too, not just for her dad."

There are many such opportunities for you to share in the lives of your stepchildren. And the investment will pay rich dividends in your relationship with them. Quality time with children of any age fosters mutual trust and respect. Problems over money, leisure time, homework, grades, peer pressure, and so on, are more easily resolved between people who have spent time together and really know one another. And what better way to get to know your stepchildren than by entering their world a few hours a week?

Consider these suggestions:

FOR ANIMAL LOVERS:

- Take a class in wildlife appreciation at the city zoo.
- Join the Audubon Society and take a class in bird-watching.
- Take horseback riding lessons.

FOR NATURE LOVERS:

- Take a gardening seminar at a local nursery.
- Enroll in a flower arranging class at a community school.
- Take a course in basic wilderness training through The Sierra Club or another environmental group.

FOR SPORTS AND GAMES FANS:
- Take a chess class.
- Sign up for golf lessons.
- Enroll in a weight-lifting or aerobics class at a local gym.

FOR SCIENCE AND TECHNOLOGY ENTHUSIASTS:
- Enroll in a computer programming course.
- Take a class in ecology, geology, or geography at night school.
- Choose a class together at a science or natural history museum.

FOR COOKS AND FOOD LOVERS:
- Take a Chinese cooking class.
- Enroll in a cake decorating class.
- Attend a lecture on health and nutrition.

FOR THE FINANCIALLY CURIOUS:
- Through a local bank find a class specializing in investments.
- Sign up for a course on stocks and bonds. These courses are sometimes sponsored by a brokerage house.
- Take a class on the history of money and banking at a community school.

FOR PERFORMERS:
- Take dancing lessons.
- Join a choir or amateur chorus open to adults and young people.
- Enroll in an acting class or public speaking course.

FOR BOOK LOVERS:
- Take a course at a local college on the history of English literature.
- Enroll in a library reading program.
- Join a book club.

Whatever you and your stepchild decide to do, approach it as a chance to learn something entirely new, to expand previous knowledge, and most importantly, to spend some healthy time together each week.

11 ◆ Share Your Interests with Your Stepchildren

A caring relationship between stepchildren and stepparents generally occurs over time, but you can help the process along. A good place to start is with hobbies and interests. When people talk about and participate in what interests them they are more likely to reveal things about themselves that might otherwise take months or years. A shared hobby or interest can foster the trust and friendship that forms the basis of a loving and intimate relationship.

If you sing, knit, play softball, hike, swim, or collect stamps, let the kids know about your interest. Then give them an opportunity to become better acquainted with you by sharing this part of your world. Together you could go to a ball game, participate in a sporting event, attend a concert, or assemble a collection.

Larry married Sylvia, a single mother of three young sons. He had been an avid hiker from the time he was a boy so one of the first things he did was introduce his stepsons to the outdoors. Larry looks at those early months of his new family life as an important time of bonding with his stepsons.

Rosemarie said she made a hit with her teenage baseball-playing stepson when she hauled out an album featuring photos of her as the lead hitter on the girl's softball team during high school.

Take Your Pick Following are some ways to share interests with your stepchildren of various ages.

PRE-SCHOOLERS
- Take them to the library.
- Read to them before bed.
- Play a game or color a picture with them.
- Share one of your favorite childhood games or books.

ELEMENTARY SCHOOL-AGE CHILDREN
- Introduce them to library programs and encourage reading.
- Share a book together, taking turns reading.
- Play a game of their choice.
- Do a craft or art project together.
- Plan, cook, and serve a meal together.
- Take them with you on a bike ride, city walk, or hike in the mountains.
- Plant a flower or vegetable garden together.

ADOLESCENTS AND TEENS
- Attend a game or outing they are involved with.
- Encourage them to invite a friend over for dinner or overnight.
- Be available to listen if they want to talk.
- Share some of your experiences or interests.
- Invite them out to dinner alone or to accompany you on an outing.

Of course each child is different and will require unique treatment. Some want to proceed slowly. Others, hungry for attention and nurturing, will be eager to share and participate. The important thing is to be sensitive to their responses yet true to your own instincts. Take some risks and see what happens. At the very worst you can admit that you made a mistake and apologize for it. By sharing our own flaws, we often endear ourselves to others.

12 ◆ Schedule Weekly Support Meetings

Some children may balk at the idea of a support meeting, but if you stress the word *support* and then demonstrate it when your family gathers, we think you'll notice the benefits almost immediately. Everyone needs support — adults and kids. And stepchildren really need it, especially during the time of transition from one lifestyle or household to another.

You can show your concern and care for the well-being of all family members by meeting together on a regular basis to talk about everything from the practical to the emotional. Encourage your stepchildren to talk about their feelings toward homework, school activities, chores, their parents in another household, and other issues and concerns that affect their lives. You may wish to initiate the discussion or conversation with a topic of your own.

For example, if you see some emotional distancing, or limited time spent on schoolwork, or an obsession with food or sports or the telephone, bring it up in a non-threatening way. Share your own feelings and concerns about the issues you've observed. Give the kids an opportunity to air their views. Guide the conversation so that all who wish to have a chance to share.

If you have a large family, it may be useful to institute the "buddy system" where two siblings or one adult and one child pair up for the week, agreeing to support one another in accomplishing their personal and work or school-related goals. The pair might pray together on a daily basis or have a bedtime chat or a morning walk 'n' talk that helps them stay closely connected to each other and focused on what they want to accomplish that week.

Topics to Consider

- Anger
- Trust
- Integrity
- Fairness
- Responsibility
- Forgiveness
- Gratitude

- School and work issues
- Friendships
- Chores
- House rules
- Needs, desires, wishes
- Goals
- Sibling or parent relationships

You can start the discussion by sharing something related to the topic you chose that happened in your life that week. Be specific. Tell how you got angry, for example, or how you were able to forgive someone who had hurt you. Or share your ideas for a family vacation, and ask for help with the planning.

Invite the children to take turns expressing something related to their lives. Be patient. Older stepchildren may feel resistant at first or reluctant to talk on this level. It may take a few weeks, but the more opportunities they have to see your willingness to share your own weaknesses and triumphs the more they will feel safe in opening up.

You can also offer the leadership role to a different family member each week. Ask for a volunteer. Encourage that person to choose a topic or pick one from a basket (that you provide) filled with ideas written on small slips of paper.

13 ◆ Welcome Complaints as Well as Compliments

There will be times when the communication and energy in your family life are on the skids. Unexpressed and unresolved upsets can build quickly in blended families where many individuals, each with a different background, come together under one roof. If anger and resentment are forbidden, they percolate under the surface, eventually spilling into relationships.

On the other hand, if these emotions are tolerated without discussion or solution, the attitude of the entire family can become negative and pessimistic in tone and expression.

What can you do about your family's need to express their upsets and yet maintain a realistic emotional balance? You can go with it — meaning you can give yourself, your stepchildren, and other family members opportunities to air their complaints as well as their compliments. You may simply let everyone express himself or herself or you may want to encourage something more. There may be serious inequities in an area of your family life that need to be looked at and addressed.

Help foster a climate that has room for ideas and suggestions. Show your stepchildren that by far you don't have all the answers. Let them know you are willing to listen, to consider, and to make changes. It's equally important for your stepchildren to know that you and your spouse have the final vote, but that they can count on you to consider their feelings and views before making decisions affecting them. Imagine how freeing that knowledge would be to any child.

You may discover that many issues will get solved with the passage of time. Others disappear as soon as the person verbalizes the feelings. Giving words to a problem often dispels the emotional charge, and as a result, it simply doesn't hurt as much or seem as important as it did.

Communication That Works

Create a household "suggestion" box. Invite your family to drop in their ideas about household management style or family rules or individual practices. This isn't the place to ambush individuals, but rather is a forum for sharing thoughts and views about life in your household. Tell family members you accept *compliments* as well as complaints!

Make a form with items to check off and a place for personal comments. Or leave blank sheets of paper and a pencil next to the box for everyone to write whatever he or she wishes. But enforce one practice. *For every complaint registered, the complainer must make a positive suggestion for change.*

For example, if a stepchild protests reminders to keep his room clean, then he must provide a specific plan for how he will maintain order without being reminded.

If someone complains about the food, maybe he'd like to suggest some new recipes or better yet, take over the kitchen one night a week.

The idea is to foster a sense of community and responsibility. It's not all right to just "sound off" and then walk away. A family can only thrive when everyone is involved in solving the problems that affect everyone else. The children begin to see that if they only register complaints they remain part of the problem. But they can become part of the solution when they offer constructive suggestions.

Encourage face-to-face communication. Tell your stepchildren that the best way to change something is to talk about it to someone who can do something about it. Complaining and slandering others behind their backs is as much of a problem as bottling up the anger. Remind them not to tell someone else what they're unwilling to say face-to-face to the person they're upset with. Even if families observed only this one rule of communication, the entire dynamics of their family life would improve radically. So would the dynamics of our workplaces, our society, and our world.

Promote honesty by being honest yourself. If you have a complaint against one of your stepchildren, go to him or her and talk it over. And if you have a praise or a compliment, go to him or her with that as well. Become willing to be vulnerable.

Help your stepchildren communicate with one another in person. Younger children have more trouble settling grievances with other younger children and therefore especially need support. They are more apt to run to a parent to fix it. Help them express their feelings aloud to the other party. Gently walk them through the process.

Example:

"Johnny, I feel angry when you grab my truck."

"Susie, I feel sad when you laugh at my coloring."

Then check to see if the other child "got" it, and ask him or her to respond to the other. When a child really hears the feelings of another he is more likely to change his behavior and respond with compassion and repentance. This does not occur as well when a parent interferes in the process that should take place between the two children.

Imagine how loved and valued your stepchildren would feel if you were willing to help them express and accept their feelings and learn to make room for the expression and acceptance of the feelings of others, as well. Our hunch is that there would be more compliments and fewer complaints around your house.

14 ◆ Acknowledge the Kids Night

Whatever your living situation — blended family in a two-parent household or a couple with visiting stepchildren — you can find a lot to celebrate and be grateful for, even in the midst of the usual problems and challenges. But many of us don't stop long enough to focus on what works and how special each of us is.

A night set aside to acknowledge one another would be a terrific way to boost family morale, rekindle intimacy, and demonstrate your appreciation. Stepchildren will be especially responsive to such an experience, since they often feel on the fringe in both households — the one where they live and the one they visit.

You and your spouse could plan and produce an evening that focuses on the children and what they mean to you. Here's a chance to make each one feel special. Make it a celebration they won't forget. Decorate the house with streamers and banners proclaiming something unique about each one.

Plan some entertainment too. Put on a funny skit, parody a favorite song, write a limerick or poem about each child, hide small favors and gifts around the house, prepare favorite foods, go out for dessert, look at home videos together.

The whole point is for each child to feel special. Observe closely their reactions to your statements of acknowledgment. Also ask each child, "What nice things would you like me to say about you?" Parents may forget or simply not see some of the areas that are important to the children. Their suggestions help you see what matters to them and also provide valuable feedback about their self-images.

15 ◆ Help Your Stepchildren Study Less as They Learn More

Nancy's stepson spends hours on homework that his sister completes in half the time. Marvin's stepdaughter rereads paragraphs and pages, but still can't answer the questions at the end of the chapter. His neighbor's son, on the other hand, finishes assignments swiftly and has time left to work on a stamp collection.

Nancy's and Marvin's stepchildren have never learned *how* to study. They stare out the window, jump up for every phone call, and run back and forth for snacks. Both Nancy and Marvin are understandably frustrated. They want to help, but they are concerned about interfering.

But being supportive of a stepchild's scholastic life can be a great way to create intimacy in your relationships. A child's emotional stress over changes in family structure and routines often shows up in their school work.

If you'd like to be a force for good in this area, consider some of the following ways to help your stepchildren study less, yet learn more! With a little planning and patience, their work will improve and they will come to trust you for guidance and encouragement. Their grades will improve. They'll soon tackle new and difficult material with confidence and develop useful habits that will last a lifetime.

Create a Proper Atmosphere for Study   Encourage your stepchildren to approach their homework with fresh minds, to avoid studying late at night, while sick or upset, or after an exciting football game. This means to study in the same place each day, whether in a specific room at a desk or in a quiet corner at a simple table. In other words, no juggling books, pencils, or paper on their laps in the middle of the kitchen floor.

Perfect conditions aren't always possible, but with some planning and your support, they can work around household distractions and make the hours they *do* have count. Help them to see that it's important to know when to quit studying, as well as when to start.

Encourage them to set aside a certain time for homework and stick to it as much as possible. They can save time by gathering the necessary notebooks, texts, pencils and paper *before* they begin. If they're concerned about missing phone calls, offer to take messages for them.

Choose Shorter Study Periods   Discuss with your stepchildren the merits of working for several short periods with breaks rather than one long period. For example, six half-hour study periods with breaks in between are more productive for most people than three full hours of studying. For long-term assignments, help the children budget their time for research, writing, and completing the final copy. Show them how waiting until the night before the deadline creates poor quality work, as well as physical and mental stress.

In addition, you may wish to share some of your related successes and failures.

When learning a foreign language or technical formulas for math and science, brief sessions are best. Slightly longer periods might be necessary for general subjects such as history and literature, which require reading and thinking about the material. But in general, short sessions help children understand the lessons more fully.

Activate Study Times   Much of what people learn passes in and out of their minds quickly unless they get involved with the information. By coupling their study periods with some related activity children retain more knowledge for a longer time. For example, they could read and analyze the material briefly, then jot down three key points they want to remember. They could list questions; then answer them aloud. "Read it, then write it" is good advice for students of any age.

Help the children make flash cards for math or science formulas, for foreign language vocabulary, or for spelling words. Use the cards for a quick quiz.

Repeat, Repeat, Repeat! Some students are satisfied after they've read their material once or twice. But that isn't enough. Help them drill several times, taking periodic breaks, then a quiz, before going back to the book. It's normal to forget, so assure them that repetition is a good thing. They needn't be afraid to overlearn. Repeating the lesson several times helps it "stick."

Review After they learn a section or a chapter, encourage the children to go over it frequently to keep it fresh in their minds. They'll find this a great help when preparing for finals. It eliminates the need to relearn and cram at the last minute. Review is an essential tool, an invaluable aid to permanent learning.

Read Successful students are usually avid readers. They read for fun and for information. Your stepchildren can acquire this useful habit by going to the library and meeting the librarian. Encourage them to read books they like and some they think they won't like. Perhaps they will discover new interests.

Everything they read adds to their storehouse of knowledge. And important quotations and information enhance term papers and reports. What they read today may serve them tomorrow.

Helping your stepchildren to develop good study habits is like making a patchwork quilt. It takes a square of your time and a thread of patience applied over and over. Start now and watch your stepchildren grow in confidence and courage in every area of their lives.

16 ◆ Pass the Hat

This exercise combines communication and creativity. Put a batch of hats in a box in the center of the room or in the middle of a table. If you don't have enough real hats, make some out of construction paper, or buy some at a used clothing or thrift store or costume shop. The collection could include:

- a baseball cap
- a sun visor
- a bonnet
- a straw hat
- a head scarf
- a graduation cap

- a top hat
- a surgeon's cap
- a chef's hat
- a nurse's cap
- a policeman's hat
- a Western hat

Start with the youngest child. Let him choose a hat from the box, put it on, then share what it feels like to wear this hat and what he'd do if he were a policeman, nurse, chef, etc. (depending on the hat chosen). Encourage him to be imaginative. For example, the child might say, "If I were a policeman I'd ride up and down the streets in a big car and if I saw somebody trying to hurt a little kid I'd grab him and put him in the car and take him to jail."

Imagine what you could learn from that statement. Your stepson might be worried about being hurt or bullied or kidnapped.

If your stepdaughter chose a baseball cap, she might reveal that she wants to be a baseball star and she wishes there were a team for girls in your town. Such sharing provides clues to what kids are dreaming of, wishing for, curious about, or even afraid of.

Adults can participate too, using the hats as a way to share your dreams and wishes, thereby giving children permission to stretch themselves beyond the norm.

Variations

- One person chooses a hat, shares, then passes the hat to the next person and so on. Each family member adds his or her perspective, which will broaden the imagination and intellectual skills of everyone present.

- Each person takes a turn choosing a different hat, sharing, then returning it to the box.

- Two people choose two different hats, then put on a spontaneous dialogue. For example, a policeman might talk to a nurse at a hospital about a victim of a car accident. A chef might take a food order from a cowboy who stopped at the neighborhood snack shop.

Such role playing and dialoguing increase verbal skills, promote spontaneous creativity, and foster interpersonal communication — all of which will be of value within as well as outside your home.

17 ♦ Ask your Stepchildren for Feedback

Mealtimes. Holidays. Bedtimes. Chores. Allowances. How are you going to handle routines and customs when you merge people from different backgrounds and families? Everyone has an opinion. And all their opinions are valuable. But in many situations, stepparents attempting to establish order and routine impose their own standards on their stepchildren without regard for the children's preferences or established habits.

You can gain valuable information by inviting their feedback. And how helpful it would be to learn more about one another in the process. Following is an activity you can participate in as a family or in pairs.

Getting Started Invite family members to meet at a time that allows everyone to be present and free to participate fully. Sit in a circle on the floor or at a table. Discuss the differences between the ways things were in the former family, the way they are now, and the way they may be as some members visit or live with other family members part of the year. Focus on one or two items per meeting. This exercise could take several discussions to complete. Depending on the ages of individuals, you may wish to talk or to give everyone a sheet of paper to write down or illustrate their answers.

Consider These

Food: Is there room for individual tastes? Can one be a vegetarian in your family? Who cooks? Is one person in charge or are the responsibilities for food shopping and preparation shared? Who cleans up after a meal? Is it okay to eat while watching television? Is every meal a sit-down affair?

Friends: Are friends welcome? Can they sleep over? If so, when? Can children sleep at a friend's house? Must parents meet new acquaintances before friendships can develop? Can friends play at your house after school? Can they join you for meals? Are friends welcome when an adult is not home?

School: What time do the children get up? Do they awaken themselves or does a parent issue a wake-up call? Who needs help with dressing and grooming and who doesn't? How do the children get to school? Do they take lunch or buy it? Who pays for purchased lunches? Who prepares brown-bag lunches? What happens if someone forgets lunch, books, musical instrument, etc.? Who do you call if there is an emergency? Do kids carry house keys?

Household: Who does what? Are chores posted? Do assignments change? Who takes over if someone is sick or out of town? What if someone doesn't do their chores? Are children paid for their help? How do kids participate if there is a professional cleaning service? Is time off ever permitted? For what reason? Who makes that decision?

Money: Who's in charge? Do kids receive an allowance? Is there a family budget? If so, will the kids know how the allotments are made? What if one person needs clothing or shoes or supplies more often than others? Does he or she earn that money? Where do kids get money for gifts, movies, camp, church, snacks, etc.? Is it all right for older children to baby-sit or hold part-time jobs outside the home? Do they keep their earnings or must they donate part to the household?

Pets: Are they welcome? Is anyone allergic to cat fur or dog hair? Can a new member of the family bring a pet from a former family? Who decides which pets and how many are allowed? Who's responsible for pet care? What happens if the pet is neglected? Who pays for pet food and vet care?

Bedtime: When is it and who decides? Is it based on age? Is reading in bed permitted? Who tucks who in at night? Are bedtime stories part of the routine? Do kids shower or bathe at night? What happens if someone gets sick during the night or can't get to sleep? What happens if younger children continually get out of bed? Can family pets sleep with family members? If so, which pet and which family member?

Celebrations: How are holidays celebrated? What happens if there are members of different faiths in the family? Who attends celebrations? For what occasions do you give gifts? Is money available for purchasing them? Does the birthday person pick a favorite meal or outing or restaurant? Or do the parents choose? Can friends as well as family join a celebration? Are kids' birthday parties okay? What happens to mark the birthday of an older child or young adult?

Lessons and equipment: Who pays for music, dance, or other lessons? Who pays for musical instruments and athletic gear? How long must you be committed to lessons? How do the kids get to their sessions? Who drives them to practice? Does everyone have to take certain lessons (such as piano) even when there is no interest? What happens when someone wants to quit? Who is responsible for a broken instrument, lost athletic shoes, missed lessons, or late practice sessions? What should be done in those cases?

Lifestyle: What does each one like best about the original family? What does each one like least? What does each one like best about this family? What does each one like least?

18 ♦ Share Books with Your Stepchildren

You can make a deep and lasting imprint on the life of your stepchildren by fostering their ability to read and encouraging their natural interest in books.

One school librarian years ago said that reading not only stimulates self-confidence in children, "but also helps them achieve a spiritual awareness, especially through fiction." Somehow a good story "helps children see the difference between good and evil, and right and wrong."

Young readers suffer, rejoice, laugh, and cry as they identify with characters who are carefully crafted by such gifted writers as Lee Roddy, Beverly Cleary, Jane Yolen, and Laura Ingalls Wilder. But books need not be specifically religious to stimulate spiritual values. The entire range of human emotions, when thoughtfully presented in fine prose and poetry, builds naturally, without pretense or sentiment, the very Christian characteristics parents wish to foster in their families.

Six Ways to Bring Books and Children Together

1. Choose reading material to match your step children's experiences, hobbies, and interests.
2. Guide your stepchildren to books that fit their ages and abilities. A librarian can help you with this.
3. Read aloud together whenever possible.
4. Encourage oral proficiency. The more comfortable a child is with spoken language the more easily he will learn and appreciate reading.

5. Visit the library often and let the children take out their own cards as soon as they can print their names clearly.

6. Encourage a love and respect for good books by building or buying bookshelves for your stepchildren's room or for a particular area of your home.

Between the covers of hundreds of books lies the potential for developing healthy goals, sound values, pride in one's heritage, and an awakening of the creative and spiritual resources within each child.

Make Reading a Family Tradition The comfortable and cozy surroundings of home invite children to share with parents, stepparents, and siblings the beauty of pictures and words on a page. This sharing can stimulate new ideas and viewpoints and evoke humor, joy, and sadness, too.

Most book-loving families agree that if this tradition is started early enough, it will soon become as important to the daily routine as shared meals and family prayers.

Something that works well in some homes is fifteen to thirty minutes of *reading-only* time before bed. After many years of this pleasant nightly ritual, your stepchildren (whether they live with you or visit on weekends) will reach for their current books as automatically as their toothbrushes — and consider reading for a while almost as important as your goodnight kiss.

And it is surprising how quickly nighttime problems, fears, and preoccupations disappear between the lines of a good story. It's probably wise to encourage children not to read scary stories at bedtime. As your stepchildren, especially the younger ones, close their books, their eyes close too.

Celebrate Life Through Books Thoughtful fiction, well-researched biographies, and fact-filled works provide a broad base that helps stepparents and children to not only celebrate life's triumphs together but deal with its tragedies, as well.

Virginia Lee's classic story, *The Magic Moth*, for example, is a poignant yet unsentimental story of the death of a child in the family. And Charlotte Zolotow's famous picture book, *William's Doll*, supports one little boy's struggle to find himself, combining warmth and humor, with appeal for readers of any age.

Books help families consciously create memories together that will strengthen the children and parents and affirm their basic affection for one another.

Activities to Stimulate Reading

1. Play word games together, such as Scrabble, anagrams, and so on.
2. Visit museums and other places of interest to broaden your stepchildren's experiences.
3. Choose a new word from the dictionary each day and use it during that day.
4. Develop hobbies from books.
5. Do simple science experiments from books.
6. Take your stepchildren to live theater presentations. This will expand their ability to visualize what they read.
7. Discuss together what you read.
8. Help your stepchildren choose an author they like, then read many of his or her works.
9. Tape a reading session and listen to it on a rainy day.
10. Take turns reading a book out loud.

Be sure to do these things together. And after a reading session, ask the children what they think and how they feel about the story. Separate their thought responses from their emotional responses. Get to the feelings and you get to the child.

Make reading the special ingredient that transforms your relationship with your stepchildren from a colorless negative into glowing color.

19 ◆ Write Love Notes

A warm and spontaneous way to express your love for your step-children is to write love notes. Surprise them with a few well-chosen words of acknowledgment and watch them respond.

- Tuck a note in a lunch bag, a sock, or a book.
- Post it in on the bathroom mirror, on the refrigerator door, or on the family bulletin board.
- Hide it under a pillow, in a shoe, or in a drawer.

One father left a note for his children each morning before he went to work. Later they were compiled in book form. Sometimes he offered fatherly advice. Other times he reflected on a topic he wanted to share with them. But most of the time he simply expressed his love and care. He later reported that he didn't want his children to grow up without knowing him, and since he was rarely home in the morning when they awakened, he kept in touch with them through these loving notes. What a legacy those children have!

As stepparents we can create our own version of this expressive idea. Oftentimes a well-chosen word at the right moment can help a child through a troubling experience, lighten a load, give reassurance. Acknowledging an achievement in this personal way builds self-esteem.

The note itself may not be as important as the fact that you thought about writing it and did.

Make It Personal The real gift is in personalizing a note for each child. You will want to adapt what you say and how you say it for different age groups. Preschoolers, for example, who don't read yet would respond to a stick drawing and a simple "I LOVE YOU" in big print.

An elementary school-age child will appreciate a short, easy-to-read note that gets right to the heart. "I'm proud of you. I love you." "You're a great kid. I feel good when you're around." "Thanks for doing the dishes. You were a big help."

Young adults will probably respond to something short and conservative. "I appreciated your help last night." "I like what you shared at dinner. It gave me something to think about. I love you." They may be a bit reserved or even suspicious, at first, but if you are sincere in what you say, and when you say it, they'll get it even if they don't show it.

You may find this a "stretch," since at times our stepchildren do not seem lovable. You may feel they couldn't care less about you or what you have to say. But there isn't a person alive who can continue to resist words of care, appreciation, acknowledgment, and love. And parts of your protective self will also dissolve in the process.

20 ♦ Build Your Stepchild's Self-image

Love expressed sincerely does more for building a healthy self-image than any other single thing. A baby who is kissed and cuddled feels the parent's love. A toddler who helps mommy water a plant or curls up in daddy's lap for a bedtime story knows he or she is special. Youngsters or teens who want to share a talent such as cooking or carpentry feel loved when a parent confirms their talent and supports them.

Some stepparents may feel that unless they lend a hand, they aren't showing enough interest. Surprisingly, that often is not true. Children look for your acknowledgment, but they also want the freedom to do it their way, to experiment, and even to make mistakes. Too often guidance becomes manipulation, analysis, over-protection, and criticism.

Agreeing, hovering, advising, and diagnosing are villains in the stepparent/stepchild relationship just as surely as are scolding, preaching, ordering, and criticizing.

Showing Your Love Love and understanding, however, have no influence unless they reach the child. Our conversations and gestures must be consistent with our feelings. Perhaps the best way to demonstrate them is to back off. Give your stepchildren time for privacy, a chance to refuel, an opportunity to experiment. You can look, listen, and respond, but avoid taking over.

When we demonstrate acceptance, some surprising effects are produced naturally. A child's personal sense of worth develops. Independence and self-direction are accelerated. The ability to deal with his own problems surfaces. The fulfillment of his potential is promoted, and he learns to handle disappointments with grace.

To support your stepchildren in developing healthy self-images, you may want to consider the following suggestions we have gleaned from our experience and from professionals in child development.

- Help the children satisfy their persistent need to find a place in your heart and in your home which will lead to their finding themselves and their place in society.

- Listen to and encourage them to express their feelings. Treat their emotions with respect and give them plenty of space to air them with you.

- Build confidence with *honest* praise. Kids can spot fawning and manipulating faster than most adults.

- Accept the *total* child — even those parts that challenge you. Each one is unique and deserves respect regardless of personal bias or personality differences.

- Give your stepchildren opportunities to exercise real responsibilities (not just busy work) that are in keeping with their ages, levels of understanding, and abilities.

- Allow for human error. Just as stepparents need space to experiment and to fail, so do our stepchildren.

The Process Continues The task is awesome and continues over the life of the relationship. But once your stepchildren begin to express their healthy identities and individualities, they will not be easily dismantled — a credit to those adults who have given them the gift of getting to know themselves.

Parental love (from stepparents as well as from natural parents) is the soil which nourishes the seed of a healthy self-image in the young. If we use it generously, they will grow in mind and body. Like flowers, their characters will take healthy root and their spirits will blossom. Your family will be better for it — and so will the world.

21 ◆ Boost Your Stepchildren's Spirituality

Families depend on each other for love and security, but many lack intimacy and warmth. Parents and children exist together under one roof but they don't really relate to one another. They don't talk or eat together on a regular basis and many lose sight of praying with and for one another. This is a challenge that blended families may face to an even greater degree. Stepparents may try to control or manipulate relationships. Stepchildren may withdraw or become moody and selfish in order to protect themselves. If you struggle with a cloudy climate at your house, consider the following suggestions that have brightened many Christian families.

Family Readings Choose one night a week or month for a family reading. Make it as short or as long as you like. Rotate leadership among the parents and older children. Toddlers can help by turning pages or holding the book. The psalms or familiar Bible stories in modern translations make a good starting place. Other subjects which appeal to many include friendship, love, suffering, happiness, and loyalty. Follow the reading with a brief discussion and conclude with a prayer or song.

Family Talk Much has been said about the lack of communication between adults and children. But often these misunderstandings are due to poor timing. Children come to their parents when they are tending a baby, resting, or worrying over a business problem. Parents too may probe their children when they are tired, upset, or preoccupied with school work.

You can remedy this by setting aside a time for talking each day.

You can chat over your evening meal, at snack time, or before bed. These informal times can bring about a sharing and cooperation between family members of all ages. At the table children and adults feel a sense of community often not available at other times.

Such shared conversations can be the springboard for important decisions relating to your spiritual lives. Young people can air their feelings about the ideals, goals, and values in their lives. Parents can discuss problems and successes in school, world news, and personal needs, as well.

Family Scrapbook   You may wish to start a scrapbook to document your blended family's spiritual milestones: dedications, baptisms, vacation Bible school, Christian camp, family retreats and so on. Fill the book with photos, fliers, awards, ribbons, certificates, and other documents that serve as visual reminders of spiritual experiences. Family members could also add notes to various pages, dating the entries and adding individual comments.

Family Projects   Collect canned goods for needy families, house a foreign student, or provide transportation to church for the elderly or infirm. You may also wish to become involved in a pet project that everyone can contribute to. You might save newspapers or glass bottles and donate them to a charity or haul them to a recycling center and use the redemption money for a mission or other spiritual cause.

Helping your blended family grow in the Spirit is an ongoing challenge. No one else will do it the same way, but the method isn't as important as the decision to do it. Becoming a spiritually fit family is an opportunity to practice Christ's principles all through the year. You may not accomplish everything, but being creative means being flexible as well. Do the things which appeal to your family and enlarge on them with ideas of your own.

The goal of an improved spiritual family life can be realized only if we work at it together. As that occurs we become more aware of ourselves, our families, our needs, and our place in the Christian world.

FUN

22 ◆ Create a Family Museum

One of our most treasured possessions is a fine old cabinet with glass doors that stands in the entryway of our home. We refer to it as "the family museum." It holds some unique and charming heirlooms including a railroad pocket watch that once belonged to Charles' father, an old razor of one of his grandfathers, some china play dishes that are more than a century old, a part of a hand-made patchwork quilt, Karen's first pair of earrings, Charles' boyhood Shirley Temple dishes, a metronome from Charles' piano-playing days, our first baby shoes and those of Karen's children, and many other items of great personal value. The cabinet itself is something of an heirloom, having once served as a bookcase in a law office.

When we were first married, Charles suggested the idea of bringing together in one place some of the treasured items that symbolize our heritage — items from both our families of origin, as well as the families we created with our former spouses.

What a great idea this has turned out to be! It has given each of us an opportunity to learn more about the other and to see and hold objects that testify to our pasts. It has also been a wonderful way to blend our families.

In addition, our collection of treasures has become a *living* museum, as we periodically add small, special things that represent the blending of our lives today. Perhaps most importantly, our museum serves as an anchor to the past as it reminds us of days that cannot be replaced, discarded, or ignored — especially in the lives of our children.

Choose a Place for Your Museum Your family museum can be anywhere you want it to be — a simple shelf in a corner, a portion of a bookcase, a specific piece of furniture or even a room designated for this purpose. Items for display may already be in your possession or may still be in the attic, basement, or closet of a member of your family. Ask around. Do some creative sleuthing.

By simply asking our mothers for them, Charles picked up an ancient water pitcher and a pink Fostoria serving set, and I received some lovely hand-painted dessert plates that belonged to my grandmother.

You're not likely to display everything you have. Some items, such as clothing, may be too awkward or bulky in size and shape for the display space you have. On the other hand, a piece of jewelry, small framed photos, a unique dish or serving piece, baby shoes, a first toy or book, or other one-of-a-kind items are just right for this purpose. Our museum has also become a conversation piece for our visitors.

Establish Your Own Family Collection Think of your museum as a place where the old and the new come together — a place for each member of your family to express some thing personal. Your children and stepchildren, for example, may enjoy displaying favorite items they've outgrown, such as embroidered baby socks, a tiny gold ring, or a favorite book or trinket. It's also important to encourage them to display items that connect them with the natural parent who is not in the current household. This might be a beloved photo or a particular item that belonged to that parent.

Such expressions are vital to stepchildren because they are likely to have feelings of fragmentation and loss. They may also feel guilt toward the parent they feel was left behind. This connection is vital to their overall relationship with both households.

Adults may wish to hold onto a treasured gift or piece of jewelry from their former marriages or add something inherited from a parent or grandparent. Karen has saved the string of pearls and the wedding and engagement rings given her by her former husband. She plans to pass them on to her daughters one day. Charles has kept some long-playing records and some serving tools from his first marriage.

The entire family may also agree to add special items that symbolize their times together. This could include a souvenir from a vacation or a family-made project.

The collection can be as personal as you wish, a symbol of your current life, as well as a testimony to your important and individual pasts.

23 ♦ Assemble a Photo Album for Each Child

Making a visual record of where each child in the family came from and where they are now provides a bridge from the former to the current living situation. This is a wonderful way to bring your blended family together and to give each child a sense of place in the new household.

Photo albums also stimulate memories, validate a child's heritage, and provide another way to strengthen the blended family. New stepchildren can share these images as a way of introducing themselves and giving insight into their lives.

Pictures also create opportunities for questions, discussion, and shared experiences. A photo album can be looked at over time. You and the children can pause and reflect and talk about the images at your own pace.

Getting Started Decide what kind of album is appropriate. If you have adult stepchildren, you may want to use a theme, such as "through the years," bringing together pictures from babyhood to adulthood.

If your stepchildren are teenagers, you might focus on their growing up years and call it "Life With Greg" or "This is Janice." You could give special pages to events and activities that are significant to that child, such as sports or dance or music.

If you have elementary school-age children in your household you could start the album on your own — as a gift — and then leave blank pages so you and your stepchild can add to it together over time.

If you have babies or toddlers, consider starting or adding to the traditional "baby book."

Many possibilities can be tailored to your particular family situation. Purchase large albums with filler pages at any greeting card or variety store or outlet.

Acquiring Hard-to-Get Photographs   Former spouses, grandparents, in-laws, and other family members are generally the guardians of early childhood photos, baby pictures, special event photos, and those of deceased relatives. Depending on your relationship with them, they may be happy to give you some of their collection, or loan the originals so you can have duplicates made.

Charles' former wife, for example, gave him half or more of the early childhood photos of their two children. Our mothers were also good resources for photos of us as babies and young children and for additional photos of our children at various stages of their lives.

Since our marriage in 1983 we have collected hundreds more, focusing on everyday times with our children, as well as holidays, vacations, and reunions.

One of the more challenging aspects of this activity is selecting the photos you wish to use. You don't need to include every picture you've snapped. You may want to make a wall collage of some of them. (We'll cover that in another section.) The idea is to choose a representative number of photos that creates the effect you wish to achieve.

For example, you probably don't need six versions of your stepson under the Christmas tree at age five! You can save the rest in a box or use for another purpose or pass on to his children when the time comes.

Share the Process   You can tackle this alone — especially if you want it to be a gift — or you can bring the stepchild on board. If you want the child involved, talk about what you want to do, how to do it, and then give him or her a chance to contribute in some way. Parents can organize and oversee the project. Older kids can make captions or titles or group photos according to a related theme. Younger children can help choose the photos and place them in order.

This activity can be a very healing time for the stepparent and stepchild as they participate in this process together. It can bring about understanding and knowledge for both adult and child and truly validate that child's presence and importance in the family.

The time spent in doing such a project may seem overwhelming in light of the busy household you live in. But don't underestimate the value of this activity and the effect it will have on your stepchildren today and on their children in years to come.

More than anything, a child needs a strong and certain sense of self that can be so easily lost in a blended family. Reticent children may feel set aside or even abandoned. Verbal youngsters may be afraid to sit quietly for fear of being overlooked. A photo album focusing on their lives can be a great source of comfort, validation, and testimony of who they are.

24 ◆ Share Your Hobby

Bring your blended family together in a meaningful way that will be fun and informative by sharing hobbies or interests. This is a good activity for any family, but is especially productive in a family where stepchildren and stepparents are getting to know one another.

Perhaps one person plays the piano or guitar. Another collects sewing thimbles or unusual bottles. Someone else might be a World War I buff. Still another person might be a quilter or a bird-watcher.

Find a way to involve everyone. Even younger members of your family can participate by sharing a special book or toy or a simple collection. For example, our five-year-old grandson, Noah, started collecting bottle caps and rubber bands and was very proud to tell us about them. And our two-and-a-half-year-old granddaughter, still a little young for a collection, could share her "dress up" clothes or the new additions to her doll house.

The idea is to share something of yourself, and a hobby is a great way to do that. Other family members will learn more about you and you will learn about them. As a result, you might discover a new interest, or acquire a new hobby.

Some shared hobbies might lead to a family vacation or special outing. For example, if one of your stepchildren is interested in Indian lore you might visit an Indian reservation. If cars or trains or story-writing or gardening are among the interests in your family, you could plant a window garden or schedule a family story time or visit a train or car museum.

Family Night This sharing activity could also be the focus of a Family

Night. It may even spark a communal hobby or activity such as a sing-a-long or a crafts night or a calligraphy-writing event.

You can probably expect some rivalry from your children and stepchildren, but it needn't be disconcerting. You and your spouse can monitor the evening, encouraging each one to share his or her hobby and then to listen to others during their turns. In some cases, the person sharing may wish to give others a chance to join in. For example, he or she could teach a song or how to fold paper into interesting objects or how to plant flower seeds.

It is so important for your stepchildren to contribute their interests and to participate actively. Without that opportunity they may feel an overwhelming sense of loss and displacement.

The possibilities for enriching your life together, and bonding your relationships more closely, often come through such serendipitous times of sharing.

25 ♦ Create New Customs... but Keep the Old

Most people, particularly children, thrive on customs and traditions. They like to anticipate the surprises they'll find in their Christmas stockings. They look forward to the special gingerbread a parent or grandparent makes for Thanksgiving. They may count on receiving their favorite meal as part of their birthday celebration.

Perhaps during the Christmas season, their family has always taken a drive down Candy Cane Lane to see the brightly lit homes on a neighborhood street. Or maybe they go shopping with a parent or grandmother for clothing and new shoes each year before school starts. Other traditions may involve a bedtime story or a yearly camp-out or participating in a holiday pageant at school or spending a weekend at Grandma's and Grandpa's every summer or attending an Advent workshop at church in the fall.

Parents in blended families face the challenge of initiating new customs, yet keeping the old ones alive, so the children, and especially the stepchildren, will not lose touch with their roots.

Talk It Over Encourage children to talk about the traditions and rituals they enjoy. Assure them that you will honor at least some of those customs in the new family setting. This alone will go a long way toward helping your stepchildren feel cared for and loved and a vital part of the new family.

For example, if a child has a favorite blanket or stuffed animal, allow him or her to keep it — even if it doesn't match the decor of the room.

If some children enjoy picking out the menu for their birthday dinner, let them carry on this tradition.

If your stepchildren are used to making holiday loaves and passing them out to neighbors, get involved with them even if you rarely bake. It's your participation that matters and your willingness to let them hold onto something dear in their lives.

Introduce Some New Customs Even as you honor the children's old traditions, you may wish to introduce some of your favorite customs or choose new ones together. For example, you might suggest eating your evening meal by candlelight. This would add a touch of elegance that children probably would love. Include them in the process — allowing them to take turns lighting the candle — and before long they will remind you if you forget!

If you wish to experience some cultural events together, you could attend the *Nutcracker Suite* ballet during the Christmas season or a *Messiah* choral presentation during Easter week. If your family enjoys the experience, go again the following year. If it's a bust, drop it and try something else. The event may fail but your being together is what matters.

Give These a Try It doesn't take long for traditions to catch on. And once they become a part of a family's profile, they take on special significance. So choose the ones that are truly meaningful, the ones that promote a healthy connection to a child's past, and the ones that speak to the needs and interests of members of the current household.

- Plan a back-to-school brunch for your children and those in the neighborhood the week before school opens.
- Attend a live production of *A Christmas Carol* during the Christmas season or watch a Christmas video together.
- Make your own valentines for friends and family.

- Take a nature walk during each of the four seasons and learn about local flora and fauna.
- Bake bread together and share with neighbors.
- Visit a nursing home once a month.
- Collect toys for the needy at Christmas.
- Serve Thanksgiving dinner at a homeless shelter.
- Sing, dance, or play games together weekly.

Make new customs, but keep the old. Like friends, one is silver and the other gold!

26 ◆ Showcase Your Blended Family's Talents

An at-home talent show is a great way to air your family's talents. It's also an opportunity for each of you to discover and appreciate one another's unique abilities.

In a blended family, an event such as this can be especially significant because it provides stepchildren and stepparents a sense of community and intimacy that can deepen their relationships. It also affirms the talents and gifts of each one, as well as his or her place in the "new" family.

Talent shows are usually associated with the performing arts: dance, music, drama, poetry reading, athletic events. But you can go beyond the familiar and include a variety of individual expressions. Consider the following ideas. And be sure to help even the youngest member find something he or she can do with a minimum of adult assistance.

Original Art This is something anyone can share—even the little ones! You might prepare for this in advance by putting together an art show of one stepchild's work. Hang contributions on the wall or on a bulletin board and, if needed, help the artist think of names for each piece. You might visit the art museum with your stepchild prior to your family show so he or she can see how paintings are hung and captioned. Imagine how broadening such an experience could be for a young artist.

You could also expand this category to include amateur photography, clay sculpture, wall murals, even collages made from cut-out magazine pictures.

Needle Crafts With the resurgence of interest in early American arts and crafts, such as weaving, quilting, needlepoint, and knitting, your stepchildren may want to express their creativity in one of these ways. They could show and describe the various stages of their work, from selecting a pattern, to choosing yarns and fabrics, to the finished product and how it can be used.

Writing Many boys and girls enjoy writing poetry or stories. If you've noticed that interest in your children or stepchildren, you can encourage them to share their writing with the family. They might also wish to read a report they wrote for a school assignment or any piece of writing they feel enthusiastic about.

Performing Arts Some members of your family may dance, play a musical instrument, sing, do gymnastics, make speeches, and so on. A family talent show is a perfect place to display that ability and to practice on a real audience. This is also an opportunity for parents and stepparents to discuss and model listening skills, eye contact, and encouragement, with both the performer and the audience.

Show and Tell This familiar form of sharing is especially popular with younger children. They can show and tell about a collection they have, a special pet, hobby, or other interest. This is another way in which siblings and stepsiblings can interact and learn from and about one another.

Dress Up Children or adults may enjoy dressing up as a character from a play, movie, or book, and then telling or reading a passage about that character.

Plays and Skits Depending on the size of your family, two or more members might want to put on a short skit or play. It could be an original script or one they find in a play book. This would be an ideal way to express humor, share a pet peeve, retell a story from the Bible, or whatever else they're interested in.

By sharing God's gifts and talents with one another, a family promotes healthy self-esteem and mutual trust — two important personal tools that everyone needs to live a productive and confident life within and outside the family.

27 ◆ Make Holidays Special

Handmade decorations, ethnic customs, foods, games, and gifts with a holiday theme are all ways to create special celebrations. But you can make them special in another way by involving your stepchildren in the planning and developing phases. Allow each of the children (school-age and up) and adults in your household to be "in charge" of one holiday for the year.

Depending on the number of people, draw names of holidays out of a box or decide based on preferences. Assign an adult or older teen to be a consultant or helper for the younger children. That person will help the child plan the celebration, from food to decorations to entertainment and activities. The child-in-charge can also enlist other family members, but he or she is the leader.

This is another rich opportunity for parents to show their children and stepchildren how much they value and respect them. Young people will learn how to see a project through from beginning to end, how to exercise leadership and creativity, how to cooperate with helpers, how to draw on their own strengths, and how to ask for help when needed.

Parents can enlarge the child's thinking by asking questions during the planning stage instead of making statements or allowing the child to have too free a hand—especially when some of the plans involve spending money.

This may seem like a lot to ask of a busy parent, but actually, it can be of great benefit both emotionally and physically. Children enter into the event with greater enthusiasm because they've had a say in what is to happen. This is also a chance for stepchildren to bring into the new home some ideas and practices that were part of the former family and to help create a sense of personal space in the new environment.

Checklist

- Decide with your family which holidays you'll make special.
- Allow each child to pick a holiday to be in charge of.
- Choose an adult or teen helper.
- Ask for volunteers to help with shopping, cooking, cleaning up, etc.
- Discuss with the child what he or she would like to accomplish.
- Organize entertainment, decorations, activities.
- Plan and shop for food.
- Prepare menu items ahead of time and freeze them.
- Celebrate the holiday, share, and clean up.

Such an activity can enlarge children, help them better see their importance in the blended family, and experience the sense of community and relationship most of them long for. And besides that, you can all have a lot of fun *together*.

28 ◆ Plan a Family Slumber Party

Most children love to do grown-up things. Some like to attend movies at night, go to restaurants that have candles and tablecloths, attend an event such as a stage play or a professional athletic game. Birthdays and other celebrations are good times for such departures from the routine. But they can also be expensive. If your blended family includes several children, you may be looking for ways to mark special events without spending a lot of money.

A family slumber party is a great solution. Kids love to sleep in Mom and Dad's room and even in their bed, if allowed to. One family we know eats a picnic supper on a blanket on the floor of the parents' bedroom, followed by a slumber party in sleeping bags.

You could even invite another family to participate in this event and hold it in a large family room. The evening could include a video movie, a songfest, card games, or an amateur talent show and homemade popcorn and lemonade. There are a number of ways to go with this idea. But the important thing is that your family is doing something creative, fun, and intimate together.

You might be surprised at how much closeness can result from such an experience. It's a way to break the rules, so to speak, in a playful way that includes children and adults. This is a chance to show your spontaneity, and to allow your stepchildren the freedom to be more expressive.

Get Everyone Involved From the youngest to the oldest, engage your children and stepchildren in the planning process. Consider their suggestions for food, for sleeping arrangements, for refreshments, and for entertainment. Older children can even be put in charge of part of the evening. For example, a young adolescent could take over the evening's activities. An older adolescent or teen could plan and serve the food. Parents might surrender all the plans, depending on the family situation, and be the guests. At another time, the parents can take the lead and invite their children to a slumber party.

Obviously the form isn't as important as the event itself. Whatever draws your family together, whatever results in a closer relationship between you and your stepchildren, and whatever fosters affection and fun are the things to choose and use.

29 ◆ Camp Out in Your Backyard

This is a variation on the family slumber party theme. Most kids love to sleep in a tent. Sometimes parents aren't as enthusiastic about the idea. But you don't have to go to the beach, forest, desert, or mountains to have an old-fashioned camp-out.

A good proving ground for this activity is your own backyard and a tent large enough for all, or a couple of smaller tents (and ground cloths), depending on the size of your family. A tent could also be made from an old sheet or blanket strung over a rope stretched between two trees or posts.

What Each Camper Needs
Sleeping bag (or quilt or heavy blankets)
Flashlight
Knife, fork, and spoon
Dish and cup
Soap and towel
Toothbrush and toothpaste
Comb
Change of clothes
Sleeping attire
Enough food for two meals

Good Grub for All Start your camp-out at dinnertime. Fix a fire on an outdoor grill or camp stove. Then prepare this easy-to-fix, easy-to-clean-up meal.

Fold a piece of aluminum foil so it is double in thickness. Take a hamburger patty or veggie burger (if there are any non-meat eaters), a few strips of shredded carrot, and several slices of peeled potato and put them inside the foil. Fold the edges tight. You can fix these food "pouches" ahead of time or let each camper prepare his own.

Cook the food pouches on the grill for about fifteen minutes. Test before serving. Add a minute or two as necessary. Serve and eat accompanied by cartons of milk or small bottles of juice. For dessert, toast marshmallows on long skewers or sticks over hot coals.

Have "seconds" on hand, as most campers have big appetites!

Fun Under the Stars Squirrel Hunt is a game that delights young children, yet older children and adults can enjoy it, as well. Hide peanuts-in-the-shell around the yard. Then blow a whistle and signal everyone to gather them as fast as they can. Whoever finds the most peanuts is the winner. The fun, of course, is in eating what you found! You can read stories, tell jokes, or sing songs, as well.

After dark play a quiet game with your flashlights. Have each person take a turn shining his or her flashlight quickly on and off something in the yard, such as a plant, a corner of the house, a flower, or some other object. The others guess what it is. The one who guesses correctly takes the next turn.

If the night is clear, you can also lie on your backs and gaze at the stars. See how many pictures you can make out of the formations you see. You might be surprised at the many shapes you and your children recognize.

At bedtime, each person rolls out his sleeping bag, changes clothes, and washes up. You may need to go indoors for a toilet break, but aside from this one trip, do everything else outdoors to stay in the spirit of a real camper.

The next morning serve a simple breakfast of cereal with fresh fruit, milk (which can be kept cold outdoors in a thermos), and bagels or rolls.

After breakfast enlist everyone's help in "breaking camp." You might post a reminder list that includes:

Roll up your sleeping bag
Gather your own equipment
Wash and pack food dishes
Help take down the tent
Collect leftover food and stray papers for the
trash

You can complete your backyard camp-out with a prayer circle and any closing comments your family members would like to share about the experience.

30 ◆ Plan a Family Buffet

Sitting down to a home-cooked meal is one of the special treasures of family life — but it's one that is often overlooked during times of unpredictable work and school schedules. That's why one mother and father we know required their family to share at least one evening meal a week — usually Sunday night — when the older kids were in junior high and high school.

"It's become a tradition," said Sally. "Now we all look forward to it. This is the one hour in the week when we know for sure that everyone will be around the table at the same time. It has also become something of a therapy session. The kids share what's been going on with them and we feel encouraged to let them in on our lives too. We often make important decisions together during these times."

If you'd like to promote more togetherness in your family, consider involving each member in a family buffet. Instead of all the work falling into the hands of one person, divide it up — from planning the menu to cleaning up the dishes. At first, you may encounter some resistance, especially from older children who don't want to be tied down. But after a few unpressured meals together we think you'll find your family eager for the next homemade buffet!

Although the food brings you together for a common experience, eating should not be emphasized over fellowship. Use this opportunity for conversation, sharing, enjoying one another, and for further intimacy between you and your stepchildren. Make it a safe place for everyone to participate at the level he or she is able. One parent could oversee the entire operation but delegate jobs as the work is needed.

Preschoolers Children as young as two, with some assistance, can set the table, wash vegetables or fruit, help roll out cookie dough or arrange cupcakes or bread on a tray.

Young School-age Children They can put the ingredients for a salad into a bowl, arrange fruit on a platter, stir the batter for cookies or cupcakes, pour drinks, prepare a simple main dish from a children's cookbook.

Adolescents Boys and girls of this age group can generally be trusted with operating the stove and oven without supervision, so they could prepare any one of a large variety of dishes that are easy to make.

Teens Young adults generally have had some exposure to cooking by the time they reach junior high so they could handle a main dish, special dessert, or vegetable or pasta casserole with little help.

Your stepchildren may have a favorite dish from their other parent's home. If so, encourage them to get the recipe and help them prepare it. Make this a safe place for each one to express himself or herself through the medium of cooking. When stepparents and stepchildren work and play together, a closeness can result that goes a long way toward building a healthy and nurturing relationship.

Exploring Options If your family enjoys this event and everyone participates, consider expanding it to include holidays and other special occasions. How nice it would be for the chief household cook to occasionally relinquish his or her role. Get everyone in on the act. Then sit back and enjoy food, fun, and fellowship together as a blended family.

31 ◆ Videotape Special Events

Camcorders have all but replaced the old home movie cameras of our youth. They're portable and more affordable than ever before, making it easy to capture nearly any event you desire. Weddings, graduations, Christmas and Thanksgiving celebrations are the most obvious. But with a little advance planning, you can also lay down on tape some of those precious moments that can catch us off-guard: a child's first steps, a visit with an aging relative in a hospital or rest home, a family meeting, a surprise party, an awards ceremony, a speech, an athletic event, a piano recital, and whatever else is special to your family.

Share the Skills and the Equipment With just a little training and encouragement, many older children in the family can become part of the "camera crew." This takes the burden off parents who are generally responsible for videotaping. It is also another opportunity to foster cooperation and support among stepsiblings.

For example, you may be planning a party following a school play. One of your older children can shoot the footage and another can be the director — in charge of setting up the scenes, enlisting the people, or choosing the candid shots that will be included. Have a backup crew, as well, so the original two can take a break and also be part of the shooting. Naturally all of this will depend on how many people you have to work with. But again, the idea is to involve as many family members as possible. When people participate they are more apt to feel part of a whole. Belonging fosters affinity and affection, essential ingredients in any stepparent/stepchild relationship.

Start a Family Video Library If your family has a keen interest in videotaping then you may enjoy the challenge of putting together a library of tapes, and cataloguing them by date, time, and event. Think of the gift this would be to each child when he is ready to leave home.

32 ◆ Plant a Garden and Share the Harvest

One teen related that her favorite hobby is gardening with her stepmother. She sounded proud to tell us that all their fresh salad greens and most vegetables come from their garden.

And her stepmother said that some of the best times between them take place while they are digging and planting and harvesting their small crop. She in turn, had helped her grandfather plant a victory garden during World War II and that had sparked her lifelong interest in growing vegetables and flowers.

Young people are especially responsive to the wonder of a seed sprouting, a bulb poking its way above the soil in early spring, and trees bearing edible fruit. They are curious about nature, eager to learn some of the secrets of producing plants and blossoms, and generally have a natural sense of harmony with nature.

Gardening is also an experience that can involve the entire family, drawing on a variety of talents.

Window or Yard If you live in a condominium, apartment, or town house, space may be limited. But that needn't stop you. You can still have a small garden — from potted herbs in a kitchen window or a row of shrubs and flowers along a fence, to a variety of indoor plants in various rooms in your home.

Your stepchildren may be even more interested if they are allowed to participate in the process of choosing the plants, and being responsible for specific tasks. You can take them along on your trips to the nursery and ask for their input when you select the seeds or bulbs.

A Time for Everything Under Heaven Gardening also creates occasions to talk about growing plants that are in harmony with the seasons. For example, strawflowers are an ideal choice to plant in early spring. They bloom from midsummer until the first frost. Then they can be cut, dried, and used for autumn decorations.

Gourds are sturdy plants that ripen in the fall, appearing in many shapes and sizes and patterns. You can paint and varnish them and use them over the years for Halloween and Thanksgiving decorations.

In addition to these bright, fun plants, a host of everyday edibles are available, such as tomatoes, corn, squash, radishes, lettuce, and beans. How wonderful it would be for you and your stepchildren to prepare a garden salad for dinner, knowing that everything came from the work of your own hands. When your bounty is more than you can use, prepare a basket of fresh greens and fruits and:

- Pass them out to neighbors and friends
- Let your stepchildren share them at school
- Prepare recipes using garden-grown foods and give as gifts

Gardening also gives you a golden opportunity to discuss with your stepchildren the miracle of growing things and the bounty of God's universe and His provision for us.

33 ◆ Serve the Kids Breakfast in Bed

Breakfast in bed is usually an adult treat. But most children enjoy it too. How much fun it would be to receive such a treat on a birthday, during an illness, or for no reason at all.

Kids could put in their order or you could serve their favorite foods without even asking. And if your blended family is newly formed and you are still getting acquainted with your stepchildren, find out what foods they like best and put them on your list. There are a number of ways to make this a truly special occasion.

Hotel-style. Make up a menu card and tell the kids to check off their preferences and the time they wish to be served (during the cook's hours only!) and hang it on the doorknob outside their rooms.

Surprise. Don't ask questions. Don't hint. Don't breathe a word. Just show up one Saturday morning with a trayful of breakfast goodies and a note that says, "I love you."

Kids Serve Kids. Take turns with younger children serving older siblings or the reverse, or boys serve girls then girls serve the boys.

Birthday Breakfast-in-bed. Start a tradition at your house. The birthday person gets breakfast in bed — featuring cold pizza, if that's a favorite dish, or the traditional early morning fare with a surprise treat of some kind.

This expression of love and care is just one more way to say, "You matter"; "You're important"; "I love you"; "You're special". It will show your stepchildren that this really is a gift of love and service, not just the usual morning fare. And in a busy household where most family members are dashing off to work and school, an occasional morning of pampering would be a lovely gift indeed.

34 ◆ Create a Birthday Tree

Christmas tree, yes! But a *birthday* tree? You bet! Kids love them. Adults love them too. This is a chance to turn an indoor or outdoor tree into a tribute to your stepchild. Load the tree with bright colored ribbons, tiny wrapped packages (chewing gum, mints, a roll of dimes, a movie ticket, etc.), or funny notes and poems that say something humorous about your stepchild.

Then after the special dinner or party, give him or her ten minutes to go through the tree, dismantling all the gifts and notes and putting them into a big box. Afterward sit in a circle and watch as he or she opens each one and reads and shares it.

This is a great opportunity for other family members to participate in making that person feel special, unique, loved, and wanted. It can be a time for good-natured humor, as well, poking playful fun at the person's idiosyncracies. For example, one sibling might give another a tube of toothpaste with a note that says, "Here, squeeze your own tube for a change." Or a child who shares a room with the birthday boy or girl might wrap up a tiny flashlight with a written comment: "A night light for a night owl. Now maybe I can get some sleep around here."

These examples can stir up related habits and foibles in other members of your family. They can also awaken everyone in a gentle and playful way to the similarities and differences that make up membership in a family. It could actually have a healing effect among stepsiblings who are still forming their relationships.

Variations on a Theme

- Give the birthday person a small indoor or outdoor tree of his or her own — a validation of the child's presence and contribution to the family. And like a living Christmas tree, a living birthday tree becomes a permanent tribute to that person.

- Donate money to a tree-planting cause in your community in honor of the birthday person.
- Take out a membership in one of the natural conservation programs that works to preserve ancient redwoods, the desert Joshua trees, or the rainforests of South America in honor of the birthday person.

A tree is a symbol of life and strength and endurance — a fitting symbol for the life and strength and enduring quality of your stepchild. And what better occasion to celebrate this life than on his or her birthday!

35 ◆ Create a Gift Calendar

Are you sometimes at a loss about what to give your stepchildren for Christmas? Especially teens whose tastes seem to change with the wind? Or younger boys and girls who appear to have more books, toys, and gadgets than they know what to do with?

Consider creating a gift of the heart that is unique, personal, special, and expresses your love. A gift calendar is easy to put together, inexpensive, and fun to give and receive. And it offers you an opportunity to spread out the giving for months to come.

Here's What You'll Need A large ready-made calendar. Purchase at a greeting card or variety store or use one of the calendars you may receive from your local bank, store, savings and loan, or other organization.

OR

Make your own calendar by hand or with a computer graphics program. (Be sure to make a copy for yourself.)

Here's What to Do
1. List twelve services or gifts you'd like to give to your stepchild (that's one for each month).
2. Choose one or more dates for each month and write in the gift or service. You can spell it out, "a night off kitchen duty," or provide a clue, "look in the hall closet," or keep it a complete surprise, "be at the front door at 6:00 p.m." You can make this as simple or complex as you like. See suggestions below.

Gift-of-the-Month Sometimes we overlook the obvious in our zeal to give our stepchildren special gifts. For example, a new pencil set beautifully wrapped could delight a younger child. A teenage girl would probably be happy to receive a new shade of lipstick. A stepson who's into sports might be delighted to receive an inexpensive cap with the name of his favorite team emblazoned on the front. Gifts needn't be expensive and services don't have to be time-consuming. Consider their interests, hobbies, talents, likes, and dislikes as you make your choices. You could also tie them to the seasons and holidays reflected on the calendar.

A Grab-bag of Gift Ideas

JANUARY
- a walk-and-talk in the snow (if you live in a cold climate)
- a new pair of mittens or a snow hat
- build a snowman or make angels in the snow
- a kid's-choice video with homemade popcorn and hot cider
- $10 in spending money

FEBRUARY
- Saturday breakfast in bed
- a new CD
- free day from chores
- a movie or museum date

MARCH
- a packet of flower seeds for a window garden
- a single rose by the bedside
- a love note in a lunch box
- a small plant for the child's room

APRIL
- a dinner and sleep-over invitation to give to a friend
- a new gadget or toy of choice under $10
- an afternoon at the park or beach
- a cookie-bake time together

MAY

- a May basket with some inexpensive goodies
- the child's favorite meal for dinner
- gift "coupon" — redeemable for a manicure, back rub, bedtime story, or any other choice you wish to offer. (Naturally, the choices will vary according to the age and gender of the child and stepparent.)

JUNE

- an outing for two (museum, ball game, walk, picnic, etc.)
- play a game, color pictures, or make a craft together
- share a couple of hours at the library or a favorite museum

JULY

- plan a Fourth of July barbecue together
- have a watermelon feast
- ride bicycles together and stop for a roadside lunch

AUGUST

- hide a small money gift in a drawer, a shoe, or under a pillow
- a small, manageable pet (goldfish, hamster, parakeet)
- a day in the mountains or at the beach

SEPTEMBER

- new shoes and/or supplies for school
- a pretty barrette, hair ribbon, scarf, or T-shirt
- fun money

OCTOBER

- a craft session together using autumn leaves
- a batch of his or her favorite homemade cookies
- a new book and a homemade bookmark

NOVEMBER
- a personal thank-you letter on Thanksgiving Day
- a poem you wrote yourself
- a small basket of dried or fresh fruit for midnight munching

DECEMBER
- a personalized ornament for the Christmas tree
- a calendar for the new year
- a Bible or book of meditations for the coming year

A gift calendar is a delightful, yet personal way of saying "I love you" all year long.

36 ◆ Plan an Outing for Two

Imagine the delight on your stepchild's face when you invite him or her on a special outing for two. Depending on the child's age, that might be a baseball game, a morning of shopping followed by lunch at a special restaurant, a play or movie, a walk along the beach, a trip to the park or playground, a tennis match, a bike ride, or a visit to a museum.

Where you go is not as important as the fact that you are doing something together. Make it special. You might issue a homemade invitation several days in advance or for older children, even weeks ahead of time. Plan part of the day to be a surprise. You could bring along a picnic lunch with his or her favorite foods, stop at a scenic spot for a view of the sunset, take photos of one another, or drop by a store and let your stepchild pick out a small gift. Use the time to chat, to observe him or her, and to reveal some things about yourself. These occasions provide uninterrupted time together that can open the way for intimacy, laughter, problem-solving, and just plain fun.

Several stepparents had great success with the following plans:

Harry knew his teenage stepdaughter, who was raised in Chicago, was a White Sox fan. So when the team came to Los Angeles where he and his new family lived, he surprised her with tickets for one of the games.

Lois works for an attorney. Knowing of her stepson's fascination with the law, she arranged for the two of them to take a tour of the courthouse, meet one of the judges, and sit in on a trial in progress.

Gretchen watched her young stepdaughter spend hours drawing

pictures and making up stories. This provided an incentive to share some of the stories she had made up when she was a child. They spent an afternoon together reading stories and making up new ones.

Go for It! If your stepchild seems reluctant to be with you or is indifferent, the time may not be right for this activity. But we believe it will come. Hang on and when you see even the smallest sign of interest or curiosity, reach out. Ask questions. Suggest an outing or event and take it from there.

Harold said his stepchildren were generally unresponsive for months after he married their mother. But when he suggested a family camping trip, they were suddenly full of questions. They had never camped before and seemed interested in the new experience. He seized this opportunity to spend some private time with each one. He took his stepson with him to look at cooking equipment. Another time he invited his stepdaughter to help him pick out a family tent.

Children are often just waiting to be asked to participate, to help, to contribute their skills or talents in some way. It's up to us to seize the moment, as Harold did, and to whisk them away for some time together—whether it's as pragmatic as a trip to the supermarket with your preschooler, or as elegant as an evening at the ballet with the young dancer in your family.

37 ◆ Capture the Birthday Person

Younger children, especially, love this surprise activity. But it can also work for some adolescents. On the morning of your stepchild's birthday, "capture" him or her out of bed, then drive or walk to the home of three or four friends, capture them (it's important to alert parents ahead of time) and bring them all back to your house for a surprise party or birthday brunch. The idea is to take the kids just as they are — without combing their hair, brushing their teeth, or changing their clothes. Ask parents to have a sack ready at the door with the items the child will need for the day (swimsuit, play clothes, shoes, toiletries, etc.) By the way, this idea works best with children of the same gender.

Instead of serving the traditional birthday cake and ice cream, try one of these ideas for a birthday brunch that can be as simple or as elaborate as you wish.

Breakfast Treasure Hunt. Hide small boxes of cereal, fresh fruit, wrapped muffins, and small cartons of milk and juice around the yard. Be sure there is enough of each item for every child present. Instruct the children that you'll count to five and then blow a whistle. At the sound of the whistle everyone is to hunt for the breakfast ingredients. The first person at the table with all five pieces wins a prize.

Cook-and-serve-yourself Buffet. Depending on the age of the children, you could set up cooking stations for omelettes, pancakes, and hot cereal with fresh fruit. Invite the children to assemble their own breakfasts.

Continental Breakfast Bar. This is probably the easiest of all. Set out a bowl of fresh fruit, such as strawberries, melon slices, and apple wedges; a basket of assorted breads, muffins, or bagels; a pitcher of orange juice; a pot of hot chocolate; and plates, cups, silverware, and napkins. Invite the young people to help themselves, then assemble on the floor in the family room, or outdoors if weather permits.

Put the birthday candles in the muffins or bagels (one for each guest), light them, then lead the guests in singing "Happy Birthday." Ask your stepchild to make a silent wish and then blow out each candle.

Then form a circle. Seat the birthday boy or girl on a chair in the center. Ask guests to take turns sharing a funny story, a birthday wish or a memory about that person. This is a time of real intimacy. It's wonderful to see how much real emotion it produces. Then let the child open gifts and play a few games with friends.

When it's time to go home, send guests on their way with a small party favor!

Afterward sit down with your stepchild and talk about the party, what it meant to him, how it felt to be treated in a special way. Encourage the child to get in touch with how much the new family cares. And allow him to air any feelings he may have regarding the way things used to be or the way they are in the home of his other parent.

38 ◆ Plan a Party with Your Stepchildren

Parties are an important part of a child's life. They're a favorite way to celebrate a birthday, holiday, victory, graduation, summer vacation. Almost any occasion will do.

But successful parties don't just happen. Entertaining is an art — but it is one that can be acquired with a little time and practice. Most children cannot put on a party without some help from a caring adult. So helping your stepchild plan a great party is another opportunity for you to be a better stepparent.

And you don't need to spend a lot of money or live in a huge house to entertain your stepchildren's friends. A get-together can be as simple as water play and cookies and punch in your backyard or driveway for the very young, a game of softball and a picnic lunch at a public park for middle-grade children, or a pizza supper and scavenger hunt for adolescents.

The important thing is that you are welcoming your stepchild's friends into your home. If your stepchild does not live with you, you can still plan a party with friends in your neighborhood. This will help him or her build a network of friends to play with when he or she visits.

The real value in planning and producing the party is your interaction with each other. If you have the time and inclination, make some of the items from scratch. For example, you could have a "theme" party, creating invitations that suggest the motif.

Pizza Party.   Sketch a pizza on a half sheet of paper and divide it into eight equal parts. Write one piece of pertinent information (time, date, location, host's name etc.) on each of the "slices."

Backyard Barbecue.   Create a chef's hat on a piece of white paper and fill in the necessary info.

Splash Party.   Make a picture of a swimming pool and print the necessary data in the center of the pool.

Back-to-school Brunch.   Draw a picture of a book jacket and fill in the details on both sides.

Depending on the age of the children involved, you can make the master copy and the children can fill in the data, or together you can draw and print and cut them out.

Then make copies of the invitation, stuff them in white or colored envelopes, and pass them out or mail them to the agreed-upon guest list.

Stand-up or Sit-down   Choose simple, nourishing foods that most kids like and are easy to prepare and serve: burgers or pizza, vegetable sticks, fresh fruit chunks, oatmeal or peanut butter cookies, fruit juice. Adjust the menu according to your budget, the age of the children, and the time and location of the party.

Sometimes refreshments could be limited to dessert — cookies and juice, yogurt pops, fresh berries and grapes in individual cups, popcorn, apple cider and brownies. Whatever you decide, be sure to get your stepchild involved. He can set the table, hose down the patio, stack the plates, cups, and plasticware, or print name tags.

Older children may enjoy a "spread" where they can assemble their own salads and sandwiches. Your stepchildren will know what their friends like and dislike. So make a point of considering their opinions when making your selections.

Teenage stepchildren may appreciate having some friends in for an elegant sit-down meal that the two of you prepare together. If you want to go all-out, dress up as a maid or butler, complete with uniform and apron or tux and tie. Use your fine china, crystal glasses, best silver, candles, and special serving bowls. Request that guests dress up for the occasion. You might be surprised at how young adults used to eating on the run, respond to an evening of fine dining in the company of good friends and family. It's not right for every group, but it is an idea worth considering. See what your stepchildren think. Their enthusiasm might surprise you. And if they pan it, well, you tried! That alone will be another step toward building an open and vulnerable relationship with them.

39 ◆ Create a Blended Family Photo Journal

A caring and effective way to give everyone—especially the children—a "sense of family" is to begin a photo journal. Take photographs of various shared activities and experiences, then put them in an album opposite a page where everyone who wishes may add a caption, a comment, a memory, or a feeling.

For example, you may group a selection of photos from a vacation, graduation, birthday celebration, or the addition of a new child to the family, whatever the case may be. Then provide space for individual journal entries. Some members may wish to write more than others. Younger children can draw a picture, make a pretty border for the page, or add colorful stickers. The idea is to participate as a family and to encourage stepchildren to feel a part of the experience by sharing their perceptions and emotions.

Customize Your Album To develop closer family identity, you can choose various experiences and activities you have shared as a blended family and make those the focus of your album. Create your own or use some of the following:

- Blended family "firsts"
    - our first weekend together
    - our first party
    - our first meal as a family

- Blended family celebrations
   Christmas, Easter, Thanksgiving, and
      other holidays
   school graduations
   victory parties
   work or school award ceremonies

- Blended family vacations
   our trip to DisneyWorld
   our week at the beach
   our harbor cruise
   our backyard camp out

If you don't have photographs of these events, cut out pictures from magazines that resemble the event described, then add written captions and comments.

What's Next? Use a family mealtime to talk about plans and wishes for the coming months. Encourage all family members to find a picture in a magazine that best describes what they would like to do as a family in the future. For example, one might choose a picture of a group of people fishing or hiking. Another might want to visit another city together, and another might want to attend a certain movie or ride horses along the beach.

Make a collage of the pictures and name it (example: Flowers' Wish List). Post it on a family room or kitchen wall or bulletin board and use ideas as you plan future outings and activities. If you want to take this idea further, ask each member to write down why he or she thinks a particular activity would be fun for the whole family. Imagine the personal power and respect each child would experience in having his or her ideas and feelings so highly valued.

As you plan and participate in these events, take photos. Then add them to the photo journal.

40 ◆ Create a Family Portrait Gallery

One family we know has covered the entire wall above the stairwell to their family room with photo collages. One of Karen's sisters has devoted the wall in her hallway to family photos from her wedding day through current times. Do you have wall space you could use for this purpose?

What to include and what to exclude? That is the question. If you have a large family with older children, you may need to be more selective than a family with only one or two younger ones. You can create picture collages as these two families did, or change photos from time to time as you go through the various seasons in your life together. Retire the used ones periodically or take them out of the frames and put them into an album.

Allow your stepchildren to take part in making the choices. They may wish to include a picture of the absent parent, yet be reluctant to ask to do so. You could suggest it. What a generous invitation that would be. And how much that would mean to a child who must share his or her life with two families, two households, and two worlds. The photo wall may be the only place where they can put their birth family together in one place. If you can handle it, it would be a real gift to your stepchild.

Expand the Possibilities You could group related pictures in one place.

Vacations. Hang a collage of photos that reflect your fun times together as well as trips you've taken as a family.

School Days. This could make a great mural for an entire wall. Put up the photos you have on hand and dig out any from the past. Be sure to leave some room for those to come. You may even wish to add a photo or two from your own school days.

Just Us. Here's a chance to bring you and your stepchildren together in another way. Hanging pictures that demonstrate your togetherness further confirms the reality of your life together today. They may have to deal with the repercussions of the break- up of the family they were born into, but the more they feel a part of this new side of the family, and their place in it, the greater the healing of the past.

Wedding Wall. We have a wedding wall in our bedroom, where we have hung our photo collage from the weddings of three of our five adult children. Instead of placing the pictures in an album we would seldom look at, we chose only three from each wedding and have displayed them in frames on the wall. Every day we get to enjoy all over again the memories of those special days.

Hobbies and Athletics. All of our children have been active in sports and some have pursued hobbies, as well. From surfing to skiing, from jogging to juggling, to tumbling and tennis, we have accumulated photos of them at various times in their lives indulging in some form of fun and games. This category could be the focus of a photo gallery, as well.

Whatever your interests or pursuits or the special focus in your family, think about getting those photos out of the albums and boxes and onto the walls for all to see and enjoy and be a part of. A family gallery is more than just a parade of pictures. It's an important declaration of who you are and of the people and places and practices that are a unique expression of each one. It also gives your stepchildren the feeling that they really belong and are an important part of the family unit.

41 ◆ Learn a New Skill Together

Give yourself the gift of learning and growing together. Perhaps you and your stepchildren have always wanted to go camping. Give it a try. Call your state park system and find out what areas are available for camping and hiking. Maybe there's a group you can join so you won't be doing it alone. In some cities, for example, the Sierra Club offers FOY (Focus on Youth) weekends a couple of times a month. Some events include sleep-overs. Others are all-day hikes, treks in the desert, or weekend backpacking trips.

Maybe you'd like to take up gardening or cake decorating or pet grooming or scuba diving. Look into YMCA-sponsored events, local seminars, or training programs in the area you wish to pursue. Local newspapers sometimes advertise training opportunities from swimming to rock climbing.

Focus on learning a skill, rather than simply gathering information, so you can practice and participate together. One mother, for example, took swimming lessons along with her stepchildren. Because she had never learned as a child, they could pursue this activity together.

A stepdad who had always wanted to play chess took up this hobby with his thirteen-year-old stepson. And one family got hooked on bicycling after renting bikes on one of their vacations. Now they spend part of most weekends biking around their community for exercise and time to be together.

Community Resources Some families steer away from activities such as biking or skating or cake decorating because they assume it will put them in a financial bind. Don't let that stop you. There are an amazing number of low-priced and free resources in every community.

Check your community college system or public library for a list of resources in your areas. Consider the Sierra Club (for camping and hiking outings), Audubon Club (for bird-watching), YMCA, public park system, and church-sponsored groups for a wide variety of classes, workshops, sports and hobby groups, and other events.

For example, in San Diego alone, one can participate in camping trips for no more than carpool money and a nominal fee for renting a tent and/or backpack, if needed. Bird walks are free, arts and crafts classes are available at some parks, and church groups sponsor everything from folk dancing to sign language workshops.

If money is involved, have your family members discuss how they wish to pay for it. Let the children participate in earning the funds. This is one more way to support them in becoming resourceful, creative human beings.

42 ◆ Play with Your Stepchildren

If your stepchildren are about five to eight years of age, you have probably noticed how much they respond to personal attention and time. They love it when you play with them. Simple board games, crafts, cooking projects, puppet shows, and so forth, are popular activities with this age group.

Following are some things you can do with younger stepchildren that require little money and small segments of time. Older children may enjoy participating also. They can do the crafts with you and assist little ones with their projects or coordinate and pass out supplies.

Finger Puppets
Each person will need:
1. An old glove
2. Cardboard
3. Crayons or felt-tipped pens
4. Glue

What to do:
1. Draw on a piece of cardboard the body, head, and arms of the person or animal puppet you want.
2. Color the drawing any way you wish.
3. Cut off the first and second fingers of the glove.
4. Cut out the drawing and glue it to the back of the glove above the cut-out fingers.
5. Your first and second fingers will be the puppet's legs.
6. Move your fingers to make the puppet walk.

Paper Bag Puppets

Each person will need:

1. A small or medium-sized paper (lunch bag or grocery bag will do) with a square bottom
2. Pieces of colored construction paper
3. Scraps of felt, lace, string, and yarn
4. Crayons or paints
5. Newspaper or tissue paper

What to do:

1. Draw a face on one side of the bag.
2. Decorate the lower half of the bag to look like a costume or uniform (fire fighter, nurse, astronaut).
3. Use yarn, cotton, or strips of paper for mustaches, hair, eyes, and nose.
4. Cut a small hole the size of your finger on each side of the bag.
5. Stuff half of the bag with crushed newspaper or tissue.
6. Tie a string around the bag just below the face and above the armholes.
7. Put your fist into the bag, pushing your first finger into the crushed paper and your thumb and second finger out the side holes.

Put on a Puppet Show If everyone is interested and time permits, consider entertaining your family or the children's friends with a puppet show.

Curtain Stage. Tape or tack a large piece of material, an old blanket, or a sheet across the bottom of a doorway or between two chairs. Stand behind the curtain and move the puppets.

Carton Puppet Stage. Cut a window in a large grocery carton. Decorate it with poster paints or crayons. If you wish, cover the opening with a small curtain. Then stand behind the window and hold up the puppets.

Producing the Show

1. Choose a poem, nursery rhyme, fairy tale, or children's play

to act out. Your librarian can help you find something simple enough for small children.
2. Give each person a part to play.
3. Move the puppet when it speaks and be sure it talks in a loud voice.
4. Puppets should talk one at a time so that everyone can follow the story.
5. Keep the show short.
6. When the performance is over, serve refreshments. Lemonade or punch and cookies are simple enough for young children to prepare with your help.

Arts and Crafts Projects A backyard crafts class is another way to play with your stepchildren. Young children love to make things and then display them or give them as gifts. Following are some traditional ideas that seem to hold ongoing appeal.

Buttermilk and Chalk Drawings

Each person will need:
1. Colored chalk
2. A big piece of drawing paper
3. A small bowl or can filled with buttermilk

What to do:
1. Dip the chalk into the buttermilk.
2. Draw with the wet chalk (pretty designs, a storybook character, a favorite place, an animal, or whatever they imagine).

Scratch Drawings These are sometimes called "backwards pictures." You make the design by taking away some of the color. Here's how they work.
1. Cover one side of a large piece of white cardboard with a dark crayon. Black, brown, and blue work best, but you can experiment with other colors too.
2. Color one way, then another, until none of the white shows through.

3. Scratch your picture, using a straight pin, nail, or needle.
4. Make the outline first.
5. Fill in the details by adding smaller scratches close together.

You may wish to make a sample of each of these or other projects you choose so children will have something specific to guide them.

OUTREACH

43 ◆ Provide a Neighborhood Service

Can you and your stepchildren type, sew, knit, write, bake, fix things, or paint? Do you have a skill that's needed or wanted in your neighborhood or community? These are some ideas you may want to consider to share your skills with those living nearby who need assistance.

Type a term paper, book report, letter, or write captions for a photo album.

Sew a button on a shirt, shorten or lengthen a hemline, mend torn clothing, repair a tear, or make a complete dress, shirt, blouse, or skirt for neighbors or friends.

Bake a favorite cake, pie, cookies, muffins, pizza, pretzels, or bread and share with others.

Write a poem, story, limerick, verse, or letter for someone who is sick or homebound.

Paint a bike, a piece of furniture, a room.

Repair a toy, a game, an old dresser, a chair, a leaky faucet.

Build a bookshelf, doghouse, storage cabinet, model car.

Knit a sweater, a scarf, a winter hat, a pair of mittens.

You and your stepchildren can list your skills, then look for places and people who could use them. Some services could be voluntary. Others might provide a way to earn money.

Be a Servant Offer your services as individuals or as a family for a whole or half day. You could set aside Saturday morning to bake or sew or spend a whole day refinishing a piece of furniture or painting a room.

Be a Teacher If your stepchildren want to involve their friends, hand them a brush, a needle and thread, a recipe and ingredients, a paint brush and bucket, and show them the way.

Be a Friend Share your skill with others. Offer a class in your backyard and enlist your stepchildren's help. Show your guests some of your accomplishments in your skilled area. If you sew or knit, display some of your work. If you are creative with wood or silver or marble, share your process with your guests and tell them how you got started. You may spark a flame of talent in them.

Be Yourself Let your stepchildren see you as the creative, talented person you are. By revealing your skills and abilities they have the opportunity to see your various facets, and to respect you as a person and as an individual apart from your role as stepmom or stepdad. Sharing and serving others promotes personal satisfaction and increased self-esteem. Working together for a common good can also result in a deep and lasting intimacy between you and your stepchildren.

44 ◆ Include Grandparents and Stepgrandparents in Family Affairs

Grandparents often feel the effects of a newly formed blended family as much as the children do. Many are sad over the breakdown of the original family. Others fear a loss of contact with their natural child, now in a new marriage, as well as the possibility of not seeing their grandchildren as often as before.

Still others have built strong relationships with the former in-law and grieve the loss of him or her from their immediate family circle.

When a divorce and subsequently a new marriage occur, grandparents feel torn between loyalties. It's a difficult and stressful time for everyone, and no less stressful for grandparents than for other family members.

But this does not have to be the experience for your family. You can take the initiative and include grandparents and stepgrandparents in family events and celebrations. You might even go to them and encourage them to share their fears and concerns so you can start over together, each one aware of his or her special place in the family.

Grandparents fill out a family, bringing a dimension of wisdom, love, care, and practical help that simply isn't available in the same way from anyone else. Children are very aware of the gift a grandparent is, and they should never be denied access to these special people.

Most grandparents have the patience and perspective necessary to help a child through a trying time. They are generally eager to listen to their grandchildren, spend time with them, read stories to the little ones, and teach, share, and participate in unique ways. Grandparents can bring out a shy child, quiet a noisy one, comfort a crying baby, whip up a meal, drive a car pool, weed the yard, or take a fussy infant for a walk when needed — even if they still have busy lives of their own.

A family is nearly always richer for cultivating relationships with grandparents and for allowing children to spend time with them. Reassure your children and stepchildren that, despite the new family arrangement, they will not lose their natural grandparents. Then follow through by inviting their grandparents to family affairs, school functions, church events.

Not every grandparent will respond favorably to your overtures. Some may hang onto hurt feelings for a time, but if you open the door and leave it open they are likely, over time, to see that you have not divorced them, that you have not shut them out of the family, that they are important and there is a place for them. And what a treasured gift this is to your stepchildren. We may not live perfect lives, but we can live preferred lives.

45 ◆ Support Your Stepchildren's Relationships with Their Natural Parents

Stepchildren often feel torn between their affection for a stepparent and their natural love and loyalty toward the parent they are not living with. One of the great concerns expressed by children of divorce is the fear of losing the parent in the other household.

Some stepparents are insensitive to this deeply rooted emotion, usually because they have their own issues to work through with the other person. That person may have hurt you in some way or there may be an awkward feeling when you're in one another's presence. This is natural and, to some extent, expected. But children shouldn't have to pay the price for the unresolved feelings between adults.

As much as you are able, encourage and foster your stepchildren's relationship with the parent in the other household. Help the children prepare for their visits with the other parent. Develop a positive viewpoint and initiate conversations with the children about their concerns before and after a visit. We're not suggesting you violate their privacy or use them to get information about the parent. But you can enter into the process with your stepchildren so they will not experience added stress. Sensing your negativity doesn't serve the child.

You can assist the children in coping with these challenges by encouraging them to keep alive their relationships with both natural parents — the one who is absent as well as the one they live with. There are exceptions to this, of course. Some parents are unknown to their children because the parent died or was removed from a child's life because of physical or substance abuse or another reason making contact unwise or impossible. But even in those difficult circumstances, children can do some things to keep the relationships alive, at least in spirit, and they may need your help. Certainly they need your affirmation and approval.

Prayer.   Encourage your stepchildren to pray for both of their parents and, if you're both willing, pray together. Don't underestimate the power of prayer. It is the most important action children can take on behalf of their parents. In some cases it is the *only* action they can exercise to keep the relationship alive. Show them how to pray, show them that you pray, and pray with them often, daily if possible. This does not have to be a big deal. A few minutes at a time is plenty.

Letters.   The art of letter-writing seems lost in today's society where the telephone, modem, fax, and camcorder dominate communication. It may take some perseverance, but you can help your stepchild see the value of writing and receiving personal letters. This is an effective and heartfelt way to keep the lines open between child and parent, especially when they live some distance apart. Help your stepchildren get into the habit of writing down the things they want to share with that parent: thoughts, ideas, feelings, concerns, interests, activities. Not only will personal letters bless the absent parent, but the child will also benefit from this opportunity to "talk to" Mom or Dad in a personal way, regardless of time and distance.

Gifts.   Your stepchildren can make and send to those who live away personal greeting cards, home-baked cookies, copies of important school papers and documents, and photos. They can also do some of the same things for the parent they live with.

Sometimes children and parents in the same home go for days without seeing or speaking with one another — not because they don't care but because of time and agendas. So it is just as important for your stepchildren to have time with their "in-house" parent as it is to have time with the parent who lives out of the house.

Events album.   Your stepchildren might enjoy putting together a scrapbook or photo album of their life and times as a gift for the absent parent. This would be an excellent way for them to share their accomplishments as well as their feelings, thoughts, and activities. Variations of this idea can be compiled and presented to the parent they live with, as well.

Time together.   Children and parents need time together, even if it is limited because of the new family structure. It may be even more crucial for that reason. Children need to know for themselves what kind of person their father or mother really is. They cannot build a relationship on the hearsay of others. They must experience each parent individually. Encourage your spouse and stepchildren to go to a movie or dinner or a ball game without you. Respect their need to talk freely about the past, if they wish to.

Your spouse may be reluctant to pursue an intimate relationship with his or her children for fear of hurting your feelings or in a way that may, at times, exclude you. Imagine the gift to your stepchildren and your spouse if you can reassure them all that they have your blessing. In turn, your spouse may then offer you the same encouragement regarding your children.

In our family, for example, Charles takes his adult children out for dinner for their birthdays. Karen does not go along. If we decide to do something for that child together it's a separate occasion.

And Karen takes short trips to visit her grown children and grandchildren without Charles. They also visit them together. But we've both realized the importance of private time with our natural children. This is one way we've supported each other as parents and supported our stepchildren in their relationship with their mother and father.

As a stepparent the important thing is to *show* you care about the children's relationship with both their natural parents and that you're not trying to take their place or oppose a caring, close relationship. Elicit your stepchildren's feelings and viewpoint if they want to talk, and respect the times when they may not want to communicate. Most children need time to make the transition from one home to the other before and after parental visits. Let them know you understand and care.

It's also important for you to stay in touch with your own thoughts, attitudes, and viewpoint, and be aware of how you're expressing yourself. Do you sound bitter, angry, jealous, impatient, reluctant, authoritarian? What are you communicating? You are now one of your stepchildren's most important role models.

Extend the Love   You can support your stepchildren in other relationships, as well. Encourage them to stay in touch with their grandparents, aunts, uncles, cousins, and others — especially those who are related to the parent who lives apart from them. This may require patience and honest communication, because sometimes the absent parent does not want the custodial parent to be involved with his or her parents and other relatives. And yet the children should not be deprived of the opportunity to continue these relationships. Sudden changes reinforce grief and guilt and make it more difficult for your stepchildren to adjust to the new family structure.

This may seem like a tall order for you, at times, but your stepchildren will probably take their cue from you and your spouse. Make it easy for them. Help them initiate and maintain contact. Everyone benefits when family members of all ages are free to develop their relationships with adults and children who are important in their lives.

These experiences will be among the most important to children, particularly when they reach adulthood. The memories will enhance the color and enrich the texture of their lives as they recall the special people who contributed to them. And if you can be a part of this process, think of what a gift you will have given to them.

46 ◆ Attend School Functions Together

Depending on the situation, some stepparents may feel reticent about attending school functions with their stepchildren. Jane M. said she feared running into the "other" parent and didn't want to make the evening awkward for her stepchild or herself. This may be a wise move, but on the other hand, what message does it send to the child?

The reality is that he or she does have an extended family now and you are part of it. If possible, and only you can assess your own situation, participate in open houses, parents' nights, holiday programs, parent-teacher conferences, and other school-related meetings. These are occasions when nothing less than *being there* will do. Sometimes our presence is the most important contribution we can make and it's important not to underestimate it.

It occurs to us that one way to avoid uncomfortable feelings, or over-stepping the boundaries of the natural parents, is to ask the children how they feel. Perhaps you can even give them the opportunity to plan the evening with you. For example, your family could enjoy a favorite meal prior to going to school or you could stop at a favorite restaurant beforehand or go out for dessert following the occasion.

If it's likely that the other parent will attend, ask your stepchildren how they would like you to fit in. When children have a voice in how to manage a potentially uneasy situation they feel respected, understood, honored, and loved. And they often come up with workable solutions that the adults in their lives may not have thought of. For example, Don S. said that he was more concerned than his stepdaughter was about the discomfort of running into her natural father at the school Christmas pageant. When he told her about it, she smiled and said simply, "Don't worry, Don. I've already told Dad you'll be there. He knows I love both of you and I want both of you there."

"Solved! Just like that," said Don, chuckling. "I was carrying around all this weight for her and here she had it figured out and handled."

Not all situations will be so smooth and workable, of course. But it's important to talk things over with your stepchildren instead of assuming a position and perhaps missing out on another opportunity to participate in an important part of their lives.

An essential part of your participation is attitude.

- Look at school functions as family events not have-to's.
- Find out what your stepchildren want and expect from you.
- Ask them what to wear and what things to watch for while there.
- Be a participant, not simply an observer, and share your observations.
- Include other children or stepchildren in the evening so they can share in one another's successes.

By supporting your stepchildren's school involvement, you are modeling parental care, approval, and acceptance. It will also strengthen your relationship with your spouse and set a healthy and caring example for all the children in your family.

47 ◆ Share Yourselves as a Family

Encourage your stepchildren to join you in reaching out to others. Your family might devote one Saturday a month to community service, or one day every couple of months, depending on your situation. The following are some ideas other families have tried with success.

HOMELESS:
- Donate books, clothing, bulk food items to a shelter in your town.
- Volunteer to read to, tutor, or play with children.
- Join the food service staff and help serve a holiday dinner.
- Assemble baskets of basic food items and deliver to a shelter.

ELDERLY:
- Attend to house plants or pets.
- Prepare and deliver a meal.
- Invite them to your home for a meal.
- Run errands for them.
- Drive them to appointments

SICK AND HOUSEBOUND:
- Bring fresh flowers.
- Pick up or deliver prescriptions.
- Visit with them.
- Read to or play a game with them.
- Write letters for them.
- Shop for food and other needed items.
- Plant a window garden.

- Clean a closet.
- Do laundry.

SINGLE PARENTS:
- Baby-sit without pay.
- Share used toys and clothing.
- Play with the children so the parent can clean or cook, etc.
- Take children to the park (with parent's permission, of course).

NEIGHBORS:
- Deliver a home-baked loaf of bread.
- Walk their dog.
- Watch their property while they're on vacation.
- Water plants and feed pets.

These activities provide valuable lessons for every member of the family. Children observe and feel, long before they verbalize. So even with the youngest children, you have an opportunity to show them *by your actions* that people are important, that everyone — both the giver and the receiver — can and does make a difference.

48 ◆ Swap or Sell for Fun and Profit

Help your stepchildren clear out their closets and clean up their rooms and make money doing it. While they're at it, you might like to do the same with your closets, garage, basement, and attic. If you've never had a garage or yard sale before, here are some proven ways to proceed.

1. Gather all the books, magazines, games, toys, posters, audio tapes, equipment, dishes, clothing, etc., that you've outgrown or no longer want.
2. Patch, mend, wash, or fix any broken or worn items.
3. Pick a time that works for your sale. Weekends and summer months seem to draw the most people.
4. Advertise in a local paper, post a notice on supermarket bulletin boards, or pass out fliers in your neighborhood. Keep your ad short and to the point, stating the type of sale, date, time, and address.
5. Choose a spot for your sale. A garage, basement, or covered patio works well in all kinds of weather. In warmer climates a driveway or a front or back yard is also a good choice.
6. Group similar items together. For example, you might have one picnic table or workbench for audio tapes, books, and posters, another for clothing and accessories, another for housewares and garden tools, and a few boxes to hold children's games and small toys.
7. Arrange items in order and allow plenty of space so shoppers can move around and find things easily.
8. Price each item fairly. You could visit a few neighborhood

sales prior to setting up your own to get a feel for pricing. Tape or pin a price tag to each item.

9. Set up a stand for handling money. One of your older step-children could serve as cashier. Use a small tablet of plain paper to keep track of sales and to issue receipts, if requested.
10. Attract customers with free lemonade.
11. Invite one of your children's friends to help if you need an extra hand. Pay a small fee or offer him or her a choice of items in exchange for the help.
12. Reduce prices at the end of the sale for quick clearance. Or you could swap them for neighbors' items. Or you may wish to donate them to a church, temple, shelter, charity, or children's hospital.

This is another opportunity to be a family in action, reaching out and working together. There's a place for each person and the proceeds can go toward something you will all enjoy or support — a special event, vacation, or charity.

Rarely can children assist their parents and stepparents in an earning experience. This is one of those rare times. And think of what a positive influence it could have on their overall experience of money and money management.

49 ◆ Organize a Holiday Gift Fair

Round up your stepchildren and their friends and help them earn money for holiday spending. They can make samples and then take orders door-to-door or display the samples at your house and invite friends to shop there. Attract customers with a colorful banner (or fliers in mailboxes) something like this:

SEE US FIRST!
HOLIDAY GIFTS
made by Jan, Bruce, Bill, and Chris
Great prices! Great gifts!
Shop early for the best selection.
Saturday, 9:00 to 12:00
Murphy's backyard

Simple Gifts The ideas here are appropriate for children 7-12. Older children may wish to offer similar services, but produce more sophisticated items of their own choosing.

Trinket Boxes: Cover used candy or shoe boxes with felt scraps. Cut and glue felt letters on top: MY THINGS or JOAN'S JUNK or LETTERS. Make a few ahead of time or take orders and personalize each box with the person's name. Charge $1 to $2 each, depending on materials and time involved.

Tool Caddy: Collect empty coffee cans. Cover them with felt, tinfoil, or scraps of colorful material. Decorate with pictures or cutouts. These are good for storing small garden or household tools. Charge 50 cents per caddy.

Pencil Pots: Follow the instructions for the tool caddy, but use frozen juice cans instead. Charge 25 cents per pot.

Flowers by You: Collect empty baby food jars. Decorate with poster paints. Fill with paper flowers, which you can make from pipe cleaners and colored construction paper. Charge 25 cents to 50 cents per jar.

Serving Trays: You can make these from strong, shallow, cardboard boxes, available at grocery stores. Decorate with odds and ends you find around the house: shells, seeds, leaves, bits of yarn, doilies, felt scraps. Protect the tray from spills by giving it a coat or two of clear shellac or plastic coating. Cut a slot in each side for carrying. Sell for 75 cents or $1 each.

Holiday Ornaments: You can make pipe-cleaner candy canes by twisting red crepe paper or ribbon around pipe cleaners bent in the shape of a candy cane. Glue ends and sell for a dime each. Cranberry or popcorn chains are also easy to make. String fresh cranberries with a needle on five feet of heavy thread. Put each chain into a plastic sack. Tie with a bright ribbon. Sell as tree decorations for 50 to 75 cents each, depending on your time, neighborhood, and the price of cranberries.

Holiday Services Try a gift-wrap booth at your fair or take this service door-to-door. Wrap gifts in assorted holiday paper and charge 75 cents for small packages and $1 or more for large ones.

Your stepchildren also might make extra money by offering a Christmas card addressing service. People would likely be happy to pay 10 cents a card to have the envelopes addressed and their stamps put on. By doing one hundred cards and envelopes, the children could earn an additional $10.

This activity can encourage your stepchildren to recognize that their ideas count — and that ideas can be the start of a nurturing relationship with working and earning one's living.

50 ◆ Write a Family Letter at Thanksgiving

Family newsletters are fairly common during the Christmas season, but few of us, if any, receive them at Thanksgiving. Yet, it's a wonderful custom to start — and another way to interact with your stepchildren. Instead of simply relating a chronology of what everyone has done during the past year, take time with your spouse and children to reflect on what you are grateful for: special people, events, personal growth, health, goods, experiences, shared times, God's protection, and so on.

How special it would be if you each included your own personal note as part of the basic letter. Children will see by example that despite the challenges and problems in life, there is much to be grateful for. And when you write them down or verbalize to others your gratitude, your blessings take on even more significance.

These are some ideas to consider.

- A Thanksgiving letter with photos enclosed. You can run off copies of the master sheet to save time and expense.
- A family photo mounted on a sheet of paper, with a greeting and acknowledgment of the person you're sending it to.
- A note sharing your feelings about Thanksgiving and counting special people (those on your list of recipients) in your life as part of your "reason for the season."
- A collage of photos and signatures with a one-line greeting at

the top. (Example: A Day to Give Thanks — For *YOU* and All Our Blessings!)

Get Creative If a letter does not appeal to you, you can still recognize this special season in some physical way — even if you keep it within your own home.

Thanksgiving Poster. Mount a large poster board in your family room or kitchen where you can look at it often. Decorate it with symbols of the day. Invite each person to add whatever he or she wants that will reflect the purpose of the season. That might be a drawing, sketch, short poem, greeting, prayer of thanks, list of blessings received.

Thanksgiving Basket. Tuck a note of thanks into a basket of fresh flowers or home-baked (or store-bought) bread or muffins and deliver to the special people in your life. Children may wish to make up their own notes and baskets for grandparents and friends.

Thanksgiving Potluck. Invite the special people in your life to a potluck meal (either on Thanksgiving Day or during the following weekend). Ask each to bring a dish to share and a scripture or poem or a list of blessings received during the year. After eating, share in pairs, small groups, or as individuals.

Thanksgiving Secrets. Gather your family in a circle and invite each one to share aloud a secret blessing he or she received during the year from someone in the family. For example, perhaps you made the kids' beds one morning when they nearly missed the school bus. You didn't realize how much they had appreciated it until they shared it during this round-robin. What a blessing! Maybe your spouse or child brought home fresh flowers unexpectedly. What a blessing! Perhaps your stepson started dinner one night when you had to work overtime. What a blessing!

The process of giving thanks can be a valuable form of communication and a true expression of intimacy among family members. So often we take favors and expressions of help for granted until we reflect on them and then acknowledge them out loud to the person who was responsible.

Again, children have the opportunity to see the adult example. Being thankful is perhaps the most profound of all human emotions. It's a form of admitting that we cannot do things alone. We must lean on God, the source of all blessings, and then acknowledge and express thanks to people who contribute to us.

51 ◆ Hold a Praise-the-Lord Party

During the Thanksgiving or Christmas season you can involve your stepchildren in a celebration of praise. This is a way to give public thanks to the Lord for blessings received. It could even become an annual affair. Following are some ideas you might want to consider as you plan your party.

Guests Invite extended family, church friends, and/or neighbors. Be sure to include children. Make your own invitations or fliers, then mail or pass them out to the people on your list. Ask each one to come with a scripture and a brief prayer, and to plan to share in a few words what God has done in his or her life in recent months.

Worship and Prayer After a time of fellowship, lead the group in worship, or ask someone else to take the leadership. Invite participants to share a pertinent scripture or to speak out in spontaneous prayers of thanksgiving. Close your praise/worship time with a familiar hymn of praise. Provide printed lyrics or project them on the wall.

Communal Sharing After eating, gather your guests together and begin the sharing. Encourage people to tell others how God has blessed their lives over the past few months. One person can lead off and then call on others, as time permits. Depending on the number of guests, people can share individually, in pairs, or in small groups. Be sure to include and encourage the children in this process.

Refreshments This could be as simple or as elaborate as you wish and it's a nice way to complete the afternoon or evening. You might consider a potluck or brown-bag supper, soup and salad bar, or just a light dessert with beverages. Food shouldn't be the emphasis, but at the same time, a meal helps bring people together and provides an opportunity for informal connection and conversation.

Guest Book As your guests leave, ask them to sign their names in a notebook or on a piece of paper, and to add any comments they may wish. This record can become a permanent reminder of this family affair. You could add to it each year if you decide to keep the tradition going.

Involve All Ages Even the young members of the family can participate. They can help serve food, or pass out napkins and silverware or song sheets. One could be in charge of the guest book. Include them in the sharing process, as well. A child's simplicity and spontaneity can be an effective spark for older people who may feel shy or reluctant to share. Children are often more in touch with their emotions than adults and can bring about intimacy more swiftly. Aside from that, a praise party is a wonderful occasion for demonstrating to your children and stepchildren the importance of giving thanks to God for all things.

52 ♦ Organize a Support Group for Blended Families

Every family can benefit from support. A blended family, however, may feel the need even more as they face issues involving stepchildren, stepparents, natural parents, and grandparents. Some of the concerns are unique to their specific family. Others are experienced by all blended families.

If, at times, you feel alone with your problems and challenges, you may want to consider organizing a support group for blended families in your area. You could pass the word to people in your church, immediate neighborhood, community social service agency, or scout troop. Or you could limit the group to families you already know.

The structure of the group can be as formal or informal as you wish. Start by holding a potluck weekend brunch, supper, or picnic, inviting those you think might be interested. Perhaps at first you could meet twice a month for one to two hours. If the interest and the need is there increase to weekly meetings. Choose a place to meet (someone's home or a church meeting room), and rotate leadership every three months so the workload doesn't fall on one person.

The agenda might include a topic for discussion, a time for individual sharing of problems, concerns, ideas, solutions, and triumphs, and a time for prayer.

Ways to Expand the Support

- *Create a buddy phone system.* Encourage members to call one another for support and prayer between meetings.
- *Organize a prayer chain.* Pass around a prayer-request and a praise-report sheet at each meeting. Individuals add their entries; others look over the list and agree to pray for at least one member during that week. If an emergency prayer request comes in between meetings, one person could volunteer to call the others to share the need and request prayer.
- *Include the children from time to time.* A family picnic, a day at the beach or ballpark, or a movie or a swim date are some ways to have fun together and to involve everyone in the family.

A family support group will provide a healthy example for your stepchildren. As they see their parents and stepparents facing and working out problems, they are likely to feel safe enough to express their needs too. As soon as the parents' group is up and running, someone may want to take on the task of organizing a support group for the children in blended families.

About the Authors

Karen O'Connor is an award-winning author of thirty books. Her most recent is *When Spending Takes the Place of Feeling*. She has also written several hundred articles that have appeared in such magazines as *Reader's Digest* and *Marriage and Family Living*. O'Connor is an experienced teacher, speaker, and writing workshop leader. She lives in San Diego, California, with her husband, Charles Flowers.

Charles Flowers knows first-hand about the challenge of blended families. He and Karen O'Connor married in 1983, and between them they have five adult children and five grandchildren. He has devoted himself to strengthening their blended family through personal contact, creative activities, family gatherings, and shared time.

Flowers is a manager for Nordstrom in San Diego, California. *52 Ways to Be A Better Stepparent* is his first book.